GOD'S PEOPLE

GOD'S PEOPLE

WEST INDIAN PENTECOSTAL
SECTS IN ENGLAND

MALCOLM J. C. CALLEY

Issued under the auspices of the
Institute of Race Relations, London

OXFORD UNIVERSITY PRESS

LONDON NEW YORK

1965

Oxford University Press, Amen House, London E.C.4

GLASGOW NEW YORK TORONTO MELBOURNE WELLINGTON
BOMBAY CALCUTTA MADRAS KARACHI LAHORE DACCA
CAPE TOWN SALISBURY NAIROBI IBADAN
KUALA LUMPUR HONG KONG

*Printed in Great Britain
by Hazell Watson & Viney Ltd
Aylesbury, Bucks*

FOREWORD

IT was in the winter of 1959-60 that Dr. Malcolm Calley approached the Institute of Race Relations with the broad idea of this book. He had done some work with the aborigines of Australia and in particular had studied the Pentecostal sects to which some of them belong. He had framed the tentative hypothesis that adherence to emotional and puritan religious groups of this kind was in part at least a compensation for rejection by the national majority; it gave the members a purpose in life and enabled them to feel superior to those who looked down on them. This he believed was the case with the Australian aborigines and he wanted to test his hypothesis by a detailed study of the Pentecostal sects which he had found were springing up among West Indian immigrants in Britain.

The project was interesting in two ways. Why should the phenomena of speaking with tongues and healing have occurred in so many different parts of the world and what are the resemblances and the differences between these various manifestations? Can they really be explained on the lines Dr. Calley suggested? But from the point of view of the Institute, the enquiry was also of importance for the light it might throw indirectly on several questions vital to an understanding of the social scene in Britain. That it would be directly related to religious behaviour would add validity to observations on other subjects and it might tell us a good deal about the extent to which the immigrants feel themselves rejected in Britain, about the likelihood of their being assimilated or integrated into the main stream of British society, about their intentions as to going back to the West Indies and the likelihood of their fulfilling these intentions. The Council of the Institute therefore agreed that we should seek a financial sponsor for Dr. Calley's study and meanwhile advance funds which would enable him to make a start. Some eight months later, the Joseph Rowntree Memorial Trust generously provided money for the entire project. I am glad to have this chance to express our warm thanks to the Trustees; I believe the result will be of value to all students of the subject.

Now that the investigation is complete, it is clear that we were right in hoping that it would pay indirect dividends. Not only has Dr. Calley suggested answers to the questions about assimilation, rejection, and future intentions, but the intimate knowledge of the immigrants which he acquired in the course of his enquiry has been useful to other enquirers, with whom he has been generous in sharing it. The Institute's Survey of Race Relations in Britain directed by Mr. Rose will certainly be the richer for Dr. Calley's experience.

But if some questions are answered, many new ones are, I think, suggested. This is a very different work from Dr. Bengt Sundkler's *Bantu Prophets in South Africa*, partly because Dr. Sundkler is a believing Christian of the Lutheran tradition, while Dr. Calley is an anthropologist to whom religion is a social and psychological pheno-menon, the reaction of man to certain environmental forces, which in a modern industrial society are mainly social and economic. By the end of his study, he has to some extent modified the formulation of his hypothesis, but he has not revised the basically determinist as-sumptions behind his approach. But some of the facts revealed by his analysis suggest that for a full explanation the assumptions as well as the whole field of reference would need to be widened.

Consider first the hypothesis regarding West Indians in Britain. Dr. Calley was inclined at first to expect that the more adverse the social environment, the more probable it was that Pentecostal sects would be strong. This is what he writes of the attraction exerted by the Pentecostal sects in Jamaica: 'In rejecting the world, members claim to be superior to it . . . Success in this world is almost synony-mous with pride and devotion to the Devil; lack of worldly success is the badge of the saint [sect member] . . . The individual confronted by grinding poverty must derive a certain satisfaction from being able to feel that he is superior to it. In addition, he finds consolation in his identification with the group, which may compensate for the in-stability of family organisation, in its turn a product of poverty and slavery.' He would, I am sure, wish to add that this opinion of Jamaica is formed at second-hand and might not stand close investiga-tion. In England, where of course his study *has* been close, Dr. Calley believes the forces are similar but not the same; 'modern England is not beset by poverty' and English—that is, white English—Pente-costal sects are already adapting themselves to 'the world' on more conformist lines. As for West Indians, they are 'economically better off in England than they were at home'. 'Nor are sect members con-spicuous for their lack of prosperity in England. The City Mission . . . has . . . more relatively prosperous members holding permanent jobs than in the West Indian community generally.' It is not then against 'grinding poverty' that the West Indians are reacting here. But the immigrant has to adjust himself to an industrial society instead of an agricultural one, to a climate he finds depressing, to new skills, to a sense of unfriendliness and rejection, to a new and puzzling attitude to skin colour, to discrimination—some actual and some imagined—over housing and employment. All these, Dr. Calley suggests, are factors in the pull exerted by the Pentecostal sects, but are not, he clearly feels, quite the whole story. This must include the strong positive element of enjoyment that the sects provide. Some members can (as Dr. Sundkler showed) here find opportunities for leadership denied them elsewhere; many exercise minor roles, all can play some part. Dr. Calley speaks of their 'intense satisfaction' and adds that 'being happy is a positive religious value'. He speaks, too, of the 'genuine affection' among members. 'Love', he writes in a passage which suggests a mild surprise, 'is not only expressed ritually; members choose one another's company rather than the company of other West Indians, they welcome one another to their homes, look after each other's children, help one another to find accommodation and work and sometimes lend or give one another money . . .' They are also extremely generous in contributing to church funds, usually paying at least a tenth of their weekly earnings into the funds of the congregation.

These points have an added interest if set alongside another passage: 'The West Indian who does not take part in religious activity says that it is because he is not "saved"; he is a "sinner". The real reason may often be an unwillingness to accept the taboos on drinking, smoking and extra-marital intercourse . . .' and also, no doubt, to make the financial contributions which the members expect. Here it seems two important questions need to be answered. The adverse social forces operate in varying degrees for all West Indian immigrants. Why do some react, not by sexual promiscuity and drunkenness—which are also sometimes thought to be a reaction to adverse forces—but by embracing a religion which involves considerable self-discipline? And why are sect members 'relatively prosperous'?

Dr. Calley does not generalise about the sociology or psychology of religion and it would be quite out of place to venture into such deep waters here. But these questions are suggested by his book. A complete theory would need to account also for the positive joy and love and—if the field is considerably extended—for martyrdom and the conversion of the well-to-do. This does not detract from the value of Dr. Calley's work; on the contrary, that he suggests fresh questions enhances it. We are all in his debt as well as in that of the Joseph Rowntree Memorial Trust.

October 1964   PHILIP MASON

AUTHOR'S PREFACE

In this book I have tried to analyse the organisational aspects of West Indian Pentecostal sects in England, and to suggests some conclusions as to their origins, functions and significance. My approach has been anthropological, not philosophical or theological. As I am not myself a member of any Christian church I feel that I have been able to approach Pentecostalism without being prejudiced by sectarian loyalties. I have not been concerned with the truth or falsity of the beliefs of my informants; I have been concerned with beliefs only in so far as they inspire or justify social action, which can be done equally efficiently by true or false beliefs. Most of my information was obtained by attendance at (and often participation in) sect meetings over a period of two years (1960–62); a description of this will be found in Appendix I, 'Research Problems and Techniques.'

As my concern has been with the present I have not endeavoured to show a rounded picture of Pentecostalism's short history, but only to give enough historical information for the reader to relate the sects I am discussing to one another and to appreciate the social environment in which they have arisen. Further historical details are to be found both among the appendices and in books cited in the bibliography.

Also in appendices will be found examples of the verbal rituals of testimony, prayer and preaching, and of talking with tongues; as my concern has been with the bearing of Pentecostal ritual on social organisation, the fission and fusion of social groups and the emergence of leaders, I have not analysed it, in detail, as ritual. My definition of ritual throughout is that of the anthropologist rather than the theologian: the word 'ritual' is used in the following pages to refer to any ceremonial activity undertaken because it is felt to be pleasing to God; this includes activities (like healing rites and some prayers) which have a magical element in that they are vaguely felt to constrain God to grant favours. It also includes those which are more purely religious in that they are directed primarily towards establishing a special mystical relationship with the deity (preaching, testifying, observing taboos, most prayers and perhaps ecstasy).

The Bible tells 'saints', sect members, what God requires of them, and they justify practically everything they do in these terms. Ideally their whole lives are acts of worship. In the final analysis rituals are performed for their own sake. They are expressions of the solidarity of the Church, a celebration of togetherness. I think this is true despite the saints' belief that their rites are directed towards achieving a comfortable location in the hereafter. Belief itself is a ritual activity an interaction between the saint and God or, in Durkheim's terms, between the saint and the deified group.

Equally, as far as doctrine is concerned, I have dealt with the social effects of doctrines rather than the doctrines themselves. I have emphasised those that are important to sect organisation rather than those that my informants, along with most Christians, would consider central to their systems of belief. For example, nearly all Pentecostal testimonies express the member's belief in God and Christ, but those beliefs are unimportant to sect organisation; much more important is belief in the reality of baptism of the Spirit or in the incompatibility of smoking tobacco and holiness.

For better or for worse, West Indian sects are going to be a feature of the English religious scene for some time to come. This examination will offer a basis for speculation as to the chances of their assimilation into the life of the community to a comparable place with established religious denominations and ultimate acceptance as a valid form of Christianity.

I would like to thank the Joseph Rowntree Memorial Trust for generously financing the project and the Institute of Race Relations for undertaking its administration. I owe a special debt of gratitude to the Director of the Institute of Race Relations, Mr. Philip Mason, for his assistance, practical advice and kindly interest. Indeed without his help the project could not have been undertaken.

I would also like to thank the various members of the Institute's staff, past and present, who have helped in a variety of ways, among them Miss Janet Evanson, Dr. Donald Wood, Miss Jennie Rice, Miss Narindar Uberoi, Miss Naomi Mosbacher, Mr. Peter Silverman, Mr. Christopher Hill, Miss Cleodie Macdonald and Miss Claire Pace. I am especially grateful to Miss Mosbacher, Miss Macdonald, Miss Pace and Mr. Hill as on their shoulders has fallen the onerous task of editing.

I am grateful to Mrs. Sheila Patterson for generously sharing with me her own research results and for providing me with introductions to those West Indian religious leaders she knew and to Miss Katrin Norris for co-operation and assistance over a number of years. I would like to thank Professor Raymond Firth of the London School of Economics for permitting me to present some of my research results as a paper in a Research Seminar in the Department of Anthropology and for valuable criticism. I am also grateful to Professor John Barnes of the Australian National University and to Dr. John Harré of the University of Otago for useful suggestions about the analysis of the data.

Thanks are due also to those clergymen of various denominations who answered my questions about West Indian participation in their congregations and provided me with information about West Indian sects in their neighbourhoods.

Finally I would like to thank the West Indian sect members themselves. It is my hope that this book will lead to better understanding of their organisations and increased tolerance towards them.

CONTENTS

ILLUSTRATIONS

I

INTRODUCTION

. . . the real function of religion is not to make us think, to enrich our knowledge, nor to add to the conceptions which we owe to science others of another origin and character, but rather, it is to make us act, to aid us to live. The believer who has communicated with his god is not merely a man who sees new truths of which the unbeliever is ignorant; he is a man who is *stronger*. He feels within him more force, either to endure the trials of existence or to conquer them. It is as though he were raised above his condition as a mere man; he believes that he is saved from evil, under whatever form he may conceive this evil.

Emile Durkheim: *Elementary Forms of the Religious Life*, trans. J. W. Swain, New York, Collier Books, 1961.

And when the day of Pentecost was fully come, they were all with one accord in one place. And suddenly there came a sound from heaven as of a rushing mighty wind, and it filled all the house where they were sitting. And there appeared unto them cloven tongues like as of fire, and it sat upon each of them. And they were all filled with the Holy Ghost, and began to speak with other tongues, as the Spirit gave them utterance.

Acts ii, 1–4.

WEST INDIANS coming to England seldom join English churches but bring their religious groups with them or develop new ones which are still firmly within the West Indian Pentecostal religious tradition.

Pentecostalism is the branch of Christianity which holds that the ecstasy of members of the very early Christian church at Jerusalem (described in Chapter 2 of the Acts of the Apostles), interpreted as possession by the Holy Ghost, remains a valid, even necessary, form of religious experience today. This ecstasy is, in all Pentecostal sects, expressed in glossolalia, 'talking with tongues', but it may be expressed in other ways as well: by ritual twitching, dancing, rolling on the ground, visions and prophecy. Other branches of Christendom hold that this kind of religious ecstasy occurred only, or mainly, in the early Church, and that the spirit of God is manifested in other ways today. To them Pentecostals are at best eccentrics and at worst dangerous heretics. The popular attitude towards them—amusement and pity tempered with scorn—is partly attributable to the low social status of their followers in most of the communities in which they exist.

Pentecostalism, in its present form, as a self-consciously separate branch of Christianity, developed during the first decade of this century in the United States, England and the Continent. These local Pentecostal traditions have remained distinct or have grown farther apart; today there are native English Pentecostal churches, American ones and Continental ones. The Caribbean Pentecostal sects can be regarded as an independent local development, though the North American influence has always been very powerful. In England today there are native English Pentecostal churches with English members and American-West Indian ones with West Indian members. The English churches have a far larger following than the West Indian ones. Nominally all the larger and some of the smaller West Indian sects in England are branches of North American ones, but this does not mean that there is much direct contact with North American headquarters, nor, as we shall see, that the constituent congregations are very firmly attached to the international organisation.

In the following chapters I am calling the religious groups under discussion 'sects' rather than 'denominations' or 'churches', although the word 'church' is the only one used by members themselves. By 'sect' I understand a religious group, within a more general religious tradition, which recruits by voluntary association. Its members come from other religious groups within the general tradition. A 'church', on the other hand, does not depend on converts for the bulk of its members, but recruits naturally, the children of members becoming members as they grow up. Since most Pentecostal churches have grown out of sects they often retain a fiction of voluntary association; members must be formally accepted by rites of salvation, baptism, confirmation and so forth.

Pentecostalism is one of the more recent of the reformist 'Holiness' movements in Christianity. Some, like the Albigensians, Lollards and Hussites, were ruthlessly and fairly successfully extirpated by the church; others, like the order founded by St. Francis, were successfully incorporated into it. Still others were neither extirpated nor incorporated, and gave rise to the major Protestant denominations of today. Like Pentecostalism these movements were concerned with revitalising Christianity for ordinary people, which implied at the same time a return, if only symbolically, to the idealised simplicity

of the early church.[1] Many of the important elements found in Pentecostalism today occurred in these too. They were accompanied by a
searching of scripture and an endeavour to achieve intense religious
experience. Also like Pentecostalism, some of them encouraged
ecstatic behaviour, which may perhaps have sometimes been manifested in glossolalia. They often encouraged actual or symbolic withdrawal from the world. Pentecostalism is not a novel departure from
the general Christian tradition; it is rather the most recent flowering
of a sub-tradition as old as Christianity itself.

Christianity in its earliest phase of development must have been
very like a modern West Indian Pentecostal sect. Its members, poor,
ill-educated people, lacking in power and influence, formed small,
scattered congregations in the Roman lands bordering the Mediterranean in very much the same way as West Indian sects form scattered
congregations in the cities of the British Isles. After the execution of
Christ, the charismatic founder, leadership devolved on a better-
educated, competent administrator who consolidated the new movement. Paul stands in the same relationship to Christianity generally as
these cond-generation leader or leaders do to the typical Pentecostal sect.

Also like modern Pentecostal sects, early Christianity was prone to
fission. It does not appear to have been a single movement recognising one central authority, but rather a loosely knit assemblage of more
or less independent congregations which later often repudiated the
central authority and broke away. Paul's complaints of heresy are
constant, and the writer of the third epistle of John sounds just like a
harassed modern Pentecostal leader when he says: 'I wrote unto the
church: but Diotrophes, who loveth to have the pre-eminence among
them, receiveth us not. Wherefore, if I come, I will remember his
deeds that he doeth, prating against us with malicious words: and not
content therewith, neither doth himself receive the brethren, and
forbiddeth them that would, and casteth them out of the church.'
(3 John 9–10)

It is likely that only a few of the Christian and quasi-Christian
sects operating in Mediterranean countries during the first few
generations after the death of Christ were mentioned in the letters of
the early leaders. They may have been as numerous as Pentecostal
sects are today. The process whereby these early sects developed into
churches took very much longer than it normally takes for a sect to

[1] The best discussion of these is Norman Cohn's *The Pursuit of the Millennium*,
London, Mercury Books (Heinemann), 1962. He traces their history down to the
Ranters of seventeenth-century England.

develop today. This may well have been due to intermittent persecution by the Roman authorities, but the absence of mass media of communication and the slowness and difficulty of travel must also have played their part. The development of unorthodox beliefs, too, must have been assisted by difficulties of communication. Heresies would have had more time to become firmly established before church leaders in distant places came to hear about them and act against them.

Just as among Pentecostal sects today only a relatively small proportion of independent congregations develop into established churches, so, in the early Christian Church, most of the independent groups appear to have become extinct, though it is possible that some of them gave rise to later heresies. We know little about the very early heresies, but the later ones, like those in modern Pentecostal sects, were often unorthodox doctrines about the Trinity. Arians and Nestorians have their modern Pentecostal counterparts even though members are unaware of this parallel.

Sects, as they develop, appear to re-live the history of Christianity as a whole, and because Christianity was once a small uninfluential sect, just as they are, its sacred writings provide ample justification for their conviction that they are close to the original Apostolic tradition. This is one claim they maintain against the established churches in which they are undoubtedly correct. The sacred writings of Christianity are tailor-made to the requirements of a religious minority. In the following chapters I shall show that there is conflict between two tendencies implicit in the organisation of a group of this kind. It usually endeavours both to turn in on itself and concentrate on the present religious needs of the minority for which it caters, and to expand into a church, broadening its membership as well as its outlook and coming to terms with the society in which it exists.

Because the New Testament is a product of a sect during a very early phase of its development it is much more difficult for a religious group, as it develops in numbers and as its members begin to play a part in a wider world, to maintain its stand on 'the Bible and the Bible alone', though many of them bravely try to do so. The fantastic organisation of some large groups, especially in the United States, is largely a reflection of this dilemma. Perhaps unfortunately for the sect developing into a less sect-like group, Christianity as a whole has only one sacred book.[2] Pentecostal sects, at least, are absolutely

---

[2] This does not apply to all sects. The Church of Jesus Christ of Latter Day Saints (the Mormons) acquired a holy book in addition to the Bible.

unwilling to accept any other Christian writings as authoritative.

West Indian Pentecostal sects re-live the early days of the church in a quite literal, almost self-conscious way. Members, called 'saints', are totally lacking in historical time-sense; the days of the Apostles to them are but yesterday and, as far as they are concerned, the two thousand intervening years of Christian history are irrelevant. Leaders see themselves as additional apostles whose churches happen to be in Brixton or Battersea or Wolverhampton instead of Ephesus or Corinth or Galatia, rather than as their successors after a vast lapse of time. In a way, congregations 'play at' the New Testament; Pentecostal ritual—and ritual is all-important—consists very largely of re-enacting the scenes it describes. Even conflict within the congregation is very much a 'New Testament game' in which the various actors see themselves as donning the garb of New Testament characters and acting out their roles.

Because of the sociological similarities of these sects to the early church, the scriptural basis of Pentecostal ritual is broader than in most well-established churches. In the latter the Gospels provide the sanctions for the main rituals, but Pentecostal sects make use of the Acts of the Apostles and the Epistles as well. The 'church' itself, in its very existence, is a ritual. It is not pleasing to God simply because of the opportunities it provides for individuals to worship him. It is pleasing to him because his word describes such groups and in forming them Christians are fulfilling the 'Word'. As I shall show in Chapter VI (p. 60 f.), the 'church', the group of worshippers, is felt to stand in a relationship to God which is additional to, and transcends, the relationships of individual members. For this reason the activities of West Indian religious leaders in forming 'churches' in England cannot be understood only in terms of group dynamics and individual strivings towards dominance and leadership. To form a church is a ritual act in its own right.

The West Indian Pentecostal sects' lack of appreciation of historical time-depth is partly due to the Messianism of the Apostolic writings. Messianism is not a dominant element in these sects, but it is sufficiently important to impede their development into churches. Undoubtedly the leaders of the early Christian church saw themselves not as establishing a religious organisation to last two thousand years but rather as hastily organising converts to await the imminent 'Second Coming'. All modern Pentecostal sects see themselves as 'latter day' movements awaiting Jesus who will come without warning 'like a thief in the night'. A belief in the imminent dissolution of the world is also a specific sanction for lack of interest in the past and the future. Pentecostal sects live for today.

Pentecostal sects (and some non-Pentecostal ones as well) generally undergo a regular process of development. In the first stage, organisation is loose, the sometimes charismatic leader is very important, and the boundaries of the group are vaguely defined. At this stage rejection of 'the world' and a refusal to compromise with it are primary values. In the second phase the group acquires more formal organisation; the original leader fades out of the picture and is replaced by less colourful, but administratively more competent people. The boundaries of the group become more sharply defined and though rejection of the world is retained as a group ideology, it progressively loses its bite. The sect is forced to compromise with the world. Being 'saved', recruitment by voluntary association, comes to be replaced by natural recruitment. If the children of members are to remain in the fold then it must tone down its zeal. If it fails to hold the young it is doomed to die slowly as its original members die; only those sects that emphasise youth work survive. Of course not all sects go through this process of development; they may refuse to compromise with the world, languish, and ultimately die. Nearly every English city has its moribund native English Pentecostal or Holiness sect, the shrunk husks of past revivals.[3]

The transition from the first phase to the second is marked by the acquisition of property. When once a sect does this its halcyon days of freedom from the world are numbered. It must operate within the property laws of the society in which it exists, and whereas before it owned property its fissions could be relatively carefree, they now become increasingly acrimonious. As the sect acquires obligations to society so it demands a say in the running of it. From being concerned only with their relationship to God, members become increasingly concerned with their relationship to society; from having predominantly ritual values, the group comes to have social ones as well. At this stage the sect is well on the way to becoming a denomination, though members will vehemently repudiate the label.

When Pentecostal sects have passed out of the first phase of their development, having acquired property and thereby a stake in the world, it seems that messianic doctrines progressively lose their relevance, even though they remain a part of official doctrine. At the

---

[3] For a detailed discussion of this in relation to British Pentecostal sects see Bryan Wilson: *Sects and Society*, London, Heinemann, 1961.

same time an interest in history is awakened; the sect now has a history and very often people competent to write about it as well.[4]

All West Indian sects in England are in an early phase of their development. They recruit by voluntary association, not naturally. This applies with equal force to the English offshoots of the large internationally organised sects with headquarters in the United States and a following in many countries of the world. Although in the United States these large groups have been operating for more than half a century, and are in some areas well-established influential 'churches', in England they are little more than a decade old. As we shall see, they differ from the small ones in the financial arrangements they make for the support of the congregation but resemble them closely in other respects. The mechanisms of congregation-building and fission are much the same for small, one-or-two-congregation sects as for large, internationally organised ones.

In establishing themselves in England, the large sects have been unable to carry over the organisation already developed in the United States, and to a somewhat lesser degree in the West Indies. They have had to start again. This is because West Indian migration to England has been a migration of individuals, not of family groups. Men came first, nearly always with the idea of working for a few years in England and then returning to the West Indies. Only later did they send for their womenfolk and children. Because of this, during the early period of the development of sects in England their membership was predominantly male, and it is only since 1961 that they have started to acquire the preponderance of female members characteristic of them in the West Indies. Under these circumstances they could recruit only by voluntary association; the demographic characteristics of the migration permitted nothing else.

In the following chapters I shall describe West Indian sects in England at one stage in their development: the earliest stage. Already, however, some of them are showing signs of becoming established, of acquiring property, broadening their basis of recruitment and coming into a closer relationship with society as a whole. This is one aspect of the process whereby West Indian migrants are becoming assimilated to English society. One would expect to find the better

---

[4] Two excellent examples are C. W. Conn's history of the Church of God, *Like a Mighty Army Moves the Church of God* (Cleveland, Church of God Publishing House, 1955) and Donald Gee's *The Pentecostal Movement* (London, Elim Publishing Company, 2nd ed., 1949).

adjusted among the immigrants in those sects which are coming to terms with their environment, in conventional English churches or without religious affiliation. But for a long time yet there will be a large residue of migrants unable to adjust, and these will seek refuge in small, world-renouncing, uncompromising sects. New ones will continue to arise to take the place of those that have disintegrated.

The only sects West Indians have brought with them to England are Pentecostal ones. Quasi-Christian sects of the Pocomania and Cumina type have not been formed in England. This is partly because in the West Indies the leaders of this type of group are middle-aged people and most of the migrants to this country have been young, but also because this type of group had passed its heyday and was in decline in Jamaica at the time migration to England from the Caribbean reached its peak.

The anti-white, millennial Ras Tafari sect which supplanted Cumina and Pocomania in Jamaica has not been imported either. This is almost certainly because its members look forward to returning to Africa and are not interested in coming to England. From time to time rather half-hearted attempts have been made to start sects of the anti-white, Ras Tafari type in England, but they have nearly always been still-born.[5] Very few English towns have a large enough Jamaican population to support a Ras Tafarian sect, so all attempts to form them have been in big cities.

To Christian Jamaicans the Ras Tafari sect is 'devilish' and Christianity's main competitor. The various Christian sects and churches, though competing with one another, recognise a common ground of belief, but they recognise no common ground whatever with Ras Tafarianism. They are alarmed at its increased influence in Jamaica over the last few years and some see Ras Tafarians lurking round every corner. Many Pentecostal migrants, believing that those who are not with them must be against them, are convinced that most young male migrants are secret Ras Tafari sympathisers, if not committed followers. This is one expression of the Pentecostal proclivity, to be discussed in Chapter VI (p. 63) for thinking the very worst of the world from which they consider themselves to have withdrawn. They must see loyalties in clear-cut terms, to God or to the Devil. There is no middle path. As in their view few migrants follow God, they must follow the Devil—and the Devil is most clearly embodied in Ras Tafari and its doctrines. The Ras Tafari bogeyman has almost

---

[5] An exception is a group in West London, which in 1964 had been operating for about three years.

the status of a mythical charter[6] among West Indian Pentecostals in England, but there is no evidence that the myth conforms at all closely to reality.

The West Indian Pentecostal sects in England are changing rapidly, and to analyse their structure both synchronic and diachronic approaches are essential. Indeed it is doubtful whether a useful distinction can be made between them. The sect congregation cannot be understood in isolation from other congregations in the immediate past. Nor can the overall group of West Indian sects be understood without reference to other Christian religious groups, present and past. The existence of a sect congregation presupposes the presence of others, just as the presence of sects presupposes the presence of a more generalised, more universally accepted religious tradition.

---

[6] I use this term in very much the same sense as Malinowski, the verbal tradition, usually the story of happenings (or supposed happenings) which provide the sanction for social behaviour, including ritual, of a human group. It is perhaps worth emphasising that the truth or falsity of a myth is of little importance in anthropological analysis; what is important is that people believe it to be true. For a concise, critical analysis of Malinowski's approach to magic and religion see S. F. Nadel: 'Malinowski on Magic and Religion' in *Man and Culture, an Evaluation of the Work of Malinowski*, ed. Raymond Firth, London, Routledge and Kegan Paul, 1957. This volume contains a bibliography of Malinowski's writings.

II

ORIGINS

1. *The United States*[1]

PENTECOSTALISM appears to have developed first in the United States, with roots deep in the American, and earlier still, the English non-conformist tradition. As the United States Constitution guarantees freedom of worship and the equality of all religious groups before the law, the legal environment has been conducive to religious hetero-geneity. An individualistic tradition has favoured religious individual-ism, so that for many a migrant from Europe the United States has been the land of religious toleration as well as the land of opportunity.

New sects were coming into being in North America before there was a United States. The 'Great Awakening' of the early 1740's set the pattern for periodic religious revivals which have continued down to the present day. These were often quite interdenominational in character: Methodists, Presbyterians and Baptists took part in the Great Western Revival of the early eighteen-hundreds. Revivals were directed towards the large proportion of the population who were not church members. Garrison, suggesting that this was more than 90 per cent, comments: 'There was probably not another country in Christendom with so small a percentage of professed Christians.'[2]

Although nearly all the ungodly were of Western European deriva-tion and so born within a general Christian tradition, in many ways American revivals had as much in common with Christian mission activities in exotic, non-Christian countries as with the regular reli-gious activities of established churches in Europe. This missionary element has always been strong in the American type of revivalistic sect; most modern sects steer a path half-way between missionary proselytisa-tion and regular church worship participated in only by members. Many West Indian sects in England, though behaving in all ways like other sects, choose to call themselves missions rather than churches.[3]

It seems that large-scale migration to the United States and the movement of population westwards led people to lose touch with the

---

[1] The main source for this chapter has been J. M. Yinger (ed.): *Religion, Society and the Individual*, New York, The Macmillan Company, 1957.

[2] See Yinger, op. cit., p. 438.   [3] See Chapters III, p. 24, IV, p. 30.

religious groups in which they had grown up. Migrants were sometimes not accepted as members of already established churches in
areas in which they settled and had to start new ones of their own
which hardly differed in beliefs from those already established in the
community.[4] Throughout American history religious revival appears
to have accompanied migration and urbanisation, the breaking up of
well-established traditional groups and attendant poverty. New religious groups have arisen as an aspect of the process whereby uprooted
populations have settled down in a new social and geographical environment.

This is as true of Negro populations as of white ones. Religion in
some form appears to have played an important part in the Negro's
adjustment to slavery, as it has in his postbellum adjustment to
migration, urbanisation and segregation. The traditional Negro
religious adjustment has been Christian, but recently non-Christian
or anti-Christian religious movements have become important:
witness the development of Garveyism, the Moorish Science Temples
between the two wars, and the more recent rise of the Black Muslims.[5]

Each wave of revival has left its residue of sects in modern American society. Many of these groups must have been still-born, not
surviving the initial revival, others died more slowly or were swallowed
by more energetic or favourably placed competitors. Most have split
since their inception. Some have steadily increased their membership
right down to the present day while others remain tiny local minorities.

Many religious groups that were typical sects earlier in their history
have now become firmly established churches with a strong central
organisation, owning a great deal of property and influential in public
affairs. Of these the three largest are the Assemblies of God, the
Church of the Nazarene, and the Church of God, all of which have
large followings outside the United States.

Within the United States the social role of such religious groups
and the kind of people who join them can vary considerably from one
part of the country to another; a church which in the south-west is
wealthy and well-established, drawing its members from all social
classes except perhaps the highest, may in California or New York
function as a sect providing an avenue of symbolic withdrawal to the
economically and socially dispossessed. It is not unusual for well-
established sects that are perhaps in the process of becoming churches
to split along social class lines; the prosperous and socially mobile no

---

[4] See Muelder's discussion of Goldschmidt's work in Yinger, op. cit., p. 482.
[5] See C. E. Lincoln, *The Black Muslims in America*, Boston, Beacon Press, 1961.

longer feel the need for the typically Pentecostal ritual withdrawal from a life that is beset by insuperable economic problems, and they seek to modify ritual and belief accordingly, to make them more like those of other, respectable churches. Excesses of Pentecostal fervour embarrass them socially, whereas these remain psychologically satisfying to poor, less educated members.[6]

The Churches of God[7]

The Church of God is but one among several Pentecostal traditions to develop in the United States during the early years of this century, and has since spread to the West Indies and thence to this country. A separate tradition centred on the West Coast led to the development of the American Assemblies of God (distinct from the English Assemblies of God) and, under the leadership of Aimee Semple McPherson, the Elim Foursquare Gospel Alliance (distinct from the English Elim Church). The Churches of God resemble other Pentecostal churches in their fundamentalism, their millennialism, their rite of total immersion baptism and their insistence on the 'baptism of the Spirit' manifested in talking with tongues. They differ from other Pentecostal churches in that they perform the rite of washing the feet of saints as an adjunct to the communion service.

Distinct from the white Churches of God but of the same tradition are the many Negro churches which have Church of God as part of their official names. These have generally been forced to assume long and complicated names because the Church of God in Tennessee has established its sole legal right to the name Church of God. In England and the West Indies the rulings of United States courts have no legal force, and therefore a great many different groups call themselves Church of God. Some of the Negro churches are all but identical in beliefs and ritual with the white Churches of God; others differ from them in ways that their members consider very significant.

Doctrinally the Churches of God fall into two groups, those that baptise in the name of the Father, Son, and Holy Ghost and those that baptise in the name of Jesus only, calling themselves 'Jesus Name' churches and called by outsiders 'Jesus Only' churches (which their members find rather offensive). To the 'Father, Son, and Holy Ghost' group the 'Jesus Name' doctrine is a dangerous heresy, while the latter's adherents speak of the others scornfully as those who 'believe in many Gods'. As will be shown in later chapters, the two

---

[6] See Goldschmidt in Yinger, op. cit., p. 484.
[7] A brief history of the Church of God will be found in Appendix II.

groups co-operate with each other very little in England, and informants agree that this is the case in the West Indies as well.

The scriptural basis of the Jesus Name doctrine is as follows: 'Father, Son, and Holy Ghost' are *titles* of the Godhead, not *names*. Even when Holy Writ mentions baptism in the name of the Father, Son and Holy Ghost, it must be interpreted as an injunction to baptise in the name of Jesus, as Jesus is the only *name* of the Godhead. Had it been intended that Christians should baptise in the *titles* of the Godhead the Bible would have said so.[8]

It is, I think, wrong to see in this doctrine a definite theological position at variance with that of other Pentecostal sects; to West Indian Pentecostals it is a ritual difference and little more than that. Although the implication of the Jesus Name doctrine is Arianism, rejection of the Trinity, very few members are theologically sophisticated enough to be aware of this. Pentecostal sects do not produce theologians; indeed their whole approach is anti-intellectual. All of them, West Indian and non-West Indian, are Christocentric, the Jesus Name ones not noticeably more so than the rest. The words 'Father, Son, and Holy Ghost' are heard in Jesus Name services as often as in the services of other Pentecostal sects. They also speak of and seek the 'gifts of the Spirit' (or 'Holy Ghost')[9] just as other sects do; never have I heard these referred to as the 'gifts of Jesus'.

The 'Jesus Name' doctrine appears to have first caused dissension among Pentecostal sects in the United States in the early nineteen twenties. There were echoes of this in England, but it never gained a large following here. Today the sole representatives of the native Jesus Name tradition are a handful of congregations in Northern Ireland. In the United States the Jesus Name sects appear to have been derived from the Church of God Pentecostal tradition rather

[8] Jesus Name sects differ among themselves over whether baptism should be in the name of 'Jesus', 'Lord Jesus' or of 'Christ Jesus'. The following from Bishop Johnson (in the pamphlet *Who is it that Defies and Challenges the Whole Religious World on these Subjects?*, Philadelphia, 1958—no publisher) illustrates the basis for these disagreements: 'There is a group that has erred from the truth and are deceived by the devil. When we received the revelation that the baptism calling the titles, Father, Son and Holy Ghost was not right, the devil used another trick by telling the people to get baptised in the name of Jesus. The Apostles never said to anyone, repent and be baptised in the name of Jesus, because they knew by the Holy Ghost that there were three named Jesus mentioned in the Bible: Jesus Christ, Jesus Justus and Bar-Jesus. When you baptise saying, I will therefore baptise you in the name Jesus, some may say, which Jesus, because there are three. But when one is baptised in the name of Jesus Christ or Lord Jesus, then you know which one you were baptised in, because there is a distinction made'.
[9] See Chapter VII, pp. 72 ff.

than from the Assemblies of God tradition, as nearly all Jesus Name sects perform the rite of washing the feet of 'saints'. Also, these sects appear to have had a special appeal for Negroes: any Jesus Name sects among West Indian migrants which have headquarters in the United States are Negro sects there. Table 1 classifies the sects followed by West Indians in England according to whether they baptise in the name of the Father, Son, and Holy Ghost or in the Name of

TABLE 1

Father, Son, and Holy Ghost	Jesus Name
Church of God	Pentecostal Churches of the World
Church of God of Prophecy	Church of the Lord Jesus Christ
New Covenant Church of God	of the Apostolic Faith
Church of God in Christ	

TABLE 2

Negro Churches	White Churches
Pentecostal Churches of the World	Church of God of Prophecy
Church of the Lord Jesus Christ	Church of God
of the Apostolic Faith	
New Covenant Church of God	
Church of God in Christ	

Jesus only. Table 2 classifies them according to whether they are, in the United States, white or Negro sects.

Table 2 shows that all but two of the churches operating in England with headquarters in the United States are Negro churches, but this does not mean that the Negro group of churches is the more important in England numerically. Here I am discussing only those sects with headquarters in the United States.[10]

At present there is a tendency for Jesus Name sects to relinquish the name Church of God; the most important one in England calls itself 'Pentecostal Churches of the World', and probably most West Indians in England think of Church of God as referring exclusively to Father, Son, and Holy Ghost sects. For the sake of convenience, 'Church of God' may be taken in this study to refer only to Father, Son and Holy Ghost sects. There is also a tendency for Jesus Name sects to make use of the word 'Apostolic' in their names and I have heard Jesus Name sects referred to collectively as 'Apostolic Churches'.

[10] Others are discussed in the next section of this chapter, and in Chapter III.

This makes for confusion with the quite distinct native English
Apostolic Churches which do not belong to the Church of God
tradition. These are offshoots of the separate English Pentecostal
tradition.[11]

Probably geography, the proximity of the Southern States to the
Caribbean, ensured that the Church of God tradition became dominant there. But in addition, the Church of God rapidly acquired a
large Negro following as well as stimulating the development of a
vast number of independent Negro sects calling themselves 'Churches
of God'. West Indian migrant workers to the United States must have
come into contact with these and played their part in disseminating
Church of God ideas of church ritual and organisation in their home
islands.

Until the post-war influx of West Indians to England the Church
of God branch of Pentecostalism did not occur here, although until
the second World War it had a small following on the Continent.

2. *The West Indies*

Pentecostalism was not transplanted fully-grown from North
America to the Caribbean. There have been ecstatic sects of a Pentecostal flavour in the British West Indies since the late eighteenth
century. American Negro Baptists played an important part in
evangelising the slaves in the British West Indies, but this was
before there were any true Pentecostal sects in the United States.
Almost immediately the missionaries complained of breakaway congregations, 'native Baptists', among whom extreme behaviour was
commonplace. American and West Indian Pentecostalism developed
hand-in-hand.

Just as North American evangelists have worked in the British
West Indies, so West Indian ones have worked in North America,
the outstanding example, of course, being Garvey. This continues to
the present day; the Kingston City Mission, whose congregations in
England I have made the subject of a detailed study during the last
two years, have congregations in New York and in California. The
development of Negro sects in the British West Indies was not directly the result of slavery. In whatever capacity Africans had come to the
Caribbean they would have been exposed to social disorganisation
and stress and would probably have reacted to this through religious
organisations. In many other parts of the world situations of social
change and stress have given rise to religious movements among

[11] See Appendix III.

populations which were not slaves. In New Zealand the Hau Hau movement[12] was a response to European settlement and the social disorganisation of the Maoris that accompanied it. A similar situation gave rise to the Sun Dance among the Plains Indians of North America. In Melanesia a new Cargo Cult[13] arises almost every year, while modern Africa is a hotbed of sectarian religious movements[14]— ranging from those concerned mainly with a magico-religious solution to the problem of living in a changing world to those which, like Mau Mau, have mainly political objects. Possibly the most important role of slavery in the West Indies was to hinder the diffusion of a detailed knowledge of Christianity to the slaves, thus stimulating them to invent their own interpretations and their own sects, on which they could base an ideology of ritual withdrawal from an inhospitable world and a system of leadership apart from that of the European slave owners.

In the British islands most of the white planters belonged to the Church of England and in the French and Spanish islands they were Roman Catholics. In general it was not the policy of the Protestant churches to evangelise the slaves; members of the clergy were often slave owners. It was believed that to educate or christianise slaves was to court rebellion.

The practice of West African religion by slaves was not encouraged either; however, probably because few plantation owners had more than the vaguest idea of what religion was like in West Africa, a great deal of religious ceremonial was conducted quite openly; slaves were permitted to dance and many dances were at least partly religious in character; there were slave festivals at Christmas and Easter.

It is doubtful whether slave religion ever followed the practices of any one African tribe and it soon acquired Christian elements. As slaves came from different tribal groups in West Africa, from Ashanti, Fanti, Ibo, Dahomey and even farther afield, there must have been a considerable blending of cultural traditions. In addition, as slaves from different areas were felt to be suitable for different kinds of

[12] This was a movement that sought to evict the British from New Zealand by force of arms. Notable among their beliefs was that followers by repeating the magical formula 'Hau Hau' became invulnerable to bullets. See S. Barton Babbage, *Hau-Hauism: An Episode in the Maori Wars*, Wellington, A. H. and A. W. Reed, 1937.

[13] The literature on Cargo Cults is immense. Possibly the best modern treatment of them is Peter Worsley's *The Trumpet Shall Sound*, London, MacGibbon and Kee, 1957.

[14] Bengt Sundkler's *Bantu Prophets in South Africa*, London, Oxford University Press, for the International African Institute, 2nd edition, 1961, describes a cross-section of these.

work, it seems unlikely that the slave population of a plantation would have been tribally homogeneous. Finally, as those sold as slaves had to be vigorous to survive the 'middle passage', it is likely that most of them were young and so less well versed in their own cultural traditions than older people would have been.

Despite the heterogeneity of tribal cultures on the plantations it was a long time before the slaves were completely cut off from Africa. Every slave transport brought new arrivals of African culture, and even after the end of the slave-trade in 1807 Africans rescued from slavers by the British Navy were often released in the islands. The likelihood that slaving would be declared illegal gave impetus to the trade between 1801 and 1807; in this period some 63,000 Africans were imported into Jamaica alone.[15] The practice of having newly arrived slaves live with already established slave families so that they could be taught plantation routine must also have furthered the transmission of African culture to those who were island-born.

In Jamaica religious activity of West African derivation came to be called Myallism. This term referred to several distinct kinds of ritual behaviour; some Myall rites were concerned with countering witchcraft (*obiah*), others with protecting the living against the spirits of the dead (*duppies*), and others with ensuring that the souls of the dead arrived safely in the afterworld. Some Myall rites appear to have been more generally concerned with ensuring the welfare of the slave community.

As economic and political leadership were in the hands of white people, the plantation owners and their employees, the only avenue of leadership open to the slaves was religion. Often the Myall leaders held responsible positions on the plantations as 'drivers' or as skilled workers, so that to some extent the pattern of religious leadership was reinforced by and integrated with the secular one. But the gulf between the slave Negro and the free white man was still very great, so that it was not unusual for the 'driver' or skilled slave to lead the others in sporadic, never successful slave rebellions. The dislike of African religion by the slave owner appears to have been the result either of a vague realisation that a religious leader could take on a secular role and challenge the ascendancy of the whites, or of the fear of magic, rather than of religious antipathy to paganism.

Until the middle of the eighteenth century no organised efforts were made to evangelise the slaves; for more than a hundred years the

[15] P. D. Curtin, *The Two Jamaicas*, Cambridge, Mass., Harvard University Press, 1955, p. 24.

only religious activity open to them was Myall in its various forms. Then in 1753 two wealthy estate owners living in England were converted by a Moravian preacher and invited Moravian missionaries to establish a mission station in Jamaica.[16] They were given about 1,000 acres in St. Elizabeth and Manchester parishes, on which they were expected to support themselves, and as there was no free labour available they were forced to become slave owners. The climate was very unhealthy and the death-rate among missionaries was high. Their following seems never to have been large, and in 1943 the Jamaica census reported only 4·1 of the population to be Moravians. Probably the Moravians' lack of success was due to their dependence on the goodwill of the planters, who were better disposed towards them than they were to other nonconformist groups. This led the slaves to suspect their *bona fides*.

The Baptist church first came to the West Indies after the American War of Independence; it was spread by American Negroes who were either freed slaves or slaves of migrants from the United States. Two of these Negroes, George Lisle and Moses Baker, in 1806 asked the English Baptists to send a minister to help them, for they were finding their increasing congregations difficult to control. Not all their followers, however, accepted the official missionaries, and early in the nineteenth century there were at least three kinds of Baptists operating in Jamaica: the orthodox ones led by missionaries from England, those who had broken away from them (initially consisting of some followers of Baker and the American Negro George Gibb), and the followers of George Lewis, an evangelising pedlar who had been a slave in Virginia. Born in Africa, he taught a doctrine containing more African elements than that of other Baptists. The position is summarised in Diagram I:

Diagram I. The Jamaican Baptist Tradition

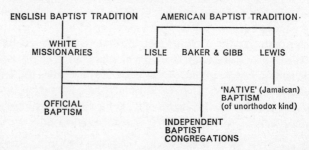

[16] Olivier, *Jamaica, the Blessed Island*, London, Faber and Faber, 1936, p. 94.

The official Baptist missionaries took over the organisation already established by their Negro predecessors: the church was organised into 'classes' and each class had a 'class leader'. As happened among the native Baptists, a class leader could easily lead his class out of the church to form a new one. Missionaries tried to curb this tendency by issuing tickets to those who attended church, who were divided into 'inquirers', 'candidates' and 'members'. Tickets costing sixpence were issued every quarter and the missionary had exclusive power to issue or withdraw them; only ticket-holders were permitted to attend church.[17] This curbed the power of the class leaders, but the missionary was still very dependent on them: he might have something like 5,000 followers in the three categories and could not be familiar with all of them.

Planters had some justification for accusing the Baptists of issuing tickets to heaven. It seems likely that the ticket itself took on ritual importance for the possessor and, since African traditions were still strong, came to be regarded as a fetish. The ticket and leader system was also used by the Methodists in Jamaica and the Church of England in Barbados.

The official Baptist missionaries and their orthodox forebears fought a constant battle against heresy. Unorthodox congregations, often led by illiterate or barely literate 'daddies', diverged from orthodoxy along several lines.[18] Some of them, perhaps because they were familiar with West African initiatory rites, overemphasised the importance of baptism, and John the Baptist, initiator-*par-excellence* of the New Testament, replaced Christ as the central figure in their mythology.[19] Perhaps because many 'daddies', being illiterate, were unable to derive doctrine directly from the Bible, and partly again because there was justification for it in traditional West African religion, much emphasis was placed on revelation. Before being accepted as a class member, the neophyte was required to have an appropriate dream, which was achieved by a fixed ritual of fasting and solitary vigil in the bush.[20]

By the first quarter of the nineteenth century possession by the Holy Ghost was an established part of native Baptist ritual. Those possessed often lay or rolled on the ground, just as their Pentecostal descendants do today. It is not clear whether 'talking with tongues', the ecstatic manifestation typical of Pentecostal sects today, had developed as early as this; it is not specifically referred to.

[17] Curtin, op. cit., p. 37. [18] Olivier, op. cit., p. 99. [19] Curtin, op. cit., p. 34.
[20] Ibid.

During the two hundred years of slavery the isolation of the plantations and the inability of the slaves to travel must have given rise to local variations in ritual, and the development of separate religious traditions. This may help to account for the sudden blossoming of sects immediately upon the introduction of Baptist Christianity.

The three traditions, Baptist, native Baptist and Myall, are influential in Jamaica at the present day—but they have not remained distinct. The Pentecostal sects probably owe most to the orthodox Baptist tradition, though their emphasis on religious ecstasy is at least partly derived from the independent Baptist sects. Possibly only ritual dancing at services derives from Myall cults, but even this is doubtful, since some English Pentecostal churches also expect their members to 'dance in the spirit'. Indeed ritual dancing as an expression of religious ecstasy has a history in Europe going back at least as far as the Protestant Reformation.

III

INTERNATIONAL LINKS

1. *Transatlantic Contacts*

ENGLAND has long had its own native Pentecostal tradition distinct from any of those existing in the United States.[1] West Indian Pentecostal sects operating in this country are independent of the native Pentecostal tradition, and spring from West Indian roots.

The immigrants brought the Churches of God with them from the West Indies.[2] They did this without seeking the blessing of one or other of the sect headquarters in the United States; they were not official emissaries. Indeed sect congregations were started here without members having any clear idea of their relationship to overseas organisations. The organisation of the congregation came first and affiliation (if any) later. Sometimes years passed before headquarters in the United States were made aware that they had acquired an English branch.

Some leaders in England have affiliated with American organisations, because doing so augments their authority. To my knowledge no American organisation has ever tried to appoint anyone other than the founder to lead congregations in England. Had they done so it is most unlikely that their nominee would have been accepted. Invariably they have confirmed the West Indian leader in England in his office of 'bishop' and conferred the title of 'overseer' or 'general overseer' on him, if he had not already assumed it. But affiliation is much less important to rank and file members. Indeed I often found that they did not know which of the Church of God organisations their congregation belonged to. This uncertainty is partly the result of a split in 1953 in the Church of God of Prophecy but is also an expression of the fluidity typical of the relationship between congregations in Jamaica. As we shall see later, it is often a matter of chance which sect an immigrant joins when he arrives in England.

There are signs that, in the future, as the sects become better established and their members more prosperous, there will be an increase in direct contact with the United States. A growing number of

---

[1] See Appendix III for a short history of British Pentecostal sects.
[2] See Appendix II.

leaders have been there since settling in England. Though this may
have the effect of tightening the control of headquarters over the
English branches, it can also be expected to have the opposite effect;
it will bring followers in England into closer touch with the turmoil of
American religious life and its heresies. This may lead to fission of
sect organisations in England. I have recorded one instance of this
happening already.

The weakness of the link of nearly all sects with the United States[3]
has had two important effects. First, it has reduced the importance of
the distinction between the larger, multi-congregational, nationally
organised sect and the small, one- or two-congregation one. Leaders
of large sects have not been backed financially from America so they
have had to face the same problems as have the leaders of smaller
ones: finding somewhere to meet, finding the rent, raising money to
buy buildings and so forth. In both the large and the small sect
organisation the local congregation is the most important unit and the
leader of a large organisation is always also the leader of a congregation. In both kinds of organisation a constituent congregation can
break away fairly easily and operate on its own.

Secondly, the distinction between Negro and white churches of
God, so important in the United States, tends to be forgotten in
England where practically all sect members are coloured. I gather
that this distinction is of little importance in Jamaica also. In
England there is a difference in the warmth of the welcome extended
to white people, but this depends mainly on the attitude of the leader.
Most of them are mildly embarrassed by the paucity of their white
members; they are prone to exaggerate their white following and their
printed handbills and programmes practically always announce hope-
fully that 'all nationalities are welcome' at their services. Nevertheless
they tacitly recognise that theirs are 'coloured churches' and feel that
their first duty is the 'coloured work', evangelising West Indians in
England. Indeed the category 'coloured people's churches' is recognised both by West Indians and religiously orientated members of the
white community. I learned that the best way to find sect congregations in the initial phases of this study was to ask for 'coloured
people's churches'. If the leaders have ambitions extending beyond
the West Indian community, it is to evangelise in the West Indies, not
among English people. Prayers are often said for the work in England

---

[3] There is one apparent exception to the rule that a sect's connections with the
    United States are tenuous; this is the Kingston City Mission, discussed in detail
    on pp. 101–2, 159–60

and Jamaica, but not even in the large sects belonging to American organisations do leaders aspire to evangelise in the United States.

Most sects maintain close contact with the West Indies, though not only with members of the same sect there. This occurs at all levels; leaders write to and receive letters from leaders in the West Indies and members communicate with their relatives and friends, many of whom belong to Church of God congregations. Some leaders, particularly those who led a congregation before emigrating, maintain a close link with a particular Jamaican congregation or a group of them, and may raise money from time to time for ' the work in Jamaica'. Except for the City Mission no sect leader in England recognises the authority of a Jamaican leader over him, although he may have done so before coming to England. The English sect organisations are felt to be distinct from those in Jamaica, not extensions of them. It is reasonable to suppose that as the West Indian community in England establishes itself contact with the West Indies will be reduced and sects will be even more independent of those at home than they are now.

2. *The City Mission*

Of the Pentecostal sects with headquarters in Jamaica which remain independent of the United States Pentecostal organisations, the only one important to this study is the Kingston City Mission, the English branches of which call themselves simply the City Mission. Whereas the early influence in other groups was from Holiness movements in North America, the City Mission was under the influence of an English Holiness movement: the Salvation Army. Like the Salvation Army it has a system of rank, but this is not pseudo-military. The highest is Bishop D.D.,[4] followed by Bishop, Light Brigade, Worker and Volunteer. Originally there were no bishops; this rank was instituted by the second leader, Mary Coore.[5] Uniforms are very much like Salvation Army ones.

The history of the City Mission is typical of sects in the West Indies; details of this history will be found in Appendix IV. Its founder Raglan Phillips appears to have been a leader of charismatic qualities who did not fit easily into any movement he did not lead himself. Three times his group began operating independently of the Salvation Army, and the third time it remained independent. This

---

[4] D.D. here stands for 'Divine Deliverer' not 'Doctor of Divinity'.
[5] Mary Coore died in June 1960 and has been succeeded by Bishop Delrose Walters.

illustrates well the ambivalence of local leaders to international religious organisations; on the one hand they feel that they stand to gain strength and prestige by joining them, but on the other hand they lose their independence.

Although Phillips was a white man, almost all his followers were coloured and drawn from among the poorer people, who rapidly imposed a typically Jamaican stamp on the movement. Although the headquarters was, and is, at the 'Ark' in Kingston, there is a large rural following, partly the result of Phillips' own revivals and partly the result of those of his successors. This following is administered from district headquarters called 'outstations'.

From being at its inception an evangelical missionary organisation the City Mission has developed into a typical Pentecostal sect. This has meant that it has had to acquire a congregation organisation parallel to the missionary one. There are now ordained City Mission ministers in Jamaica (but not in England), and congregations have 'deacons' who do not hold any of the traditional missionary ranks.

It is not unusual for Pentecostal churches to retain the name 'mission' long after they have ceased engaging much in missionary activities. The City Mission still engages in proselytisation, but to no greater extent than do other Jamaican Pentecostal sects. It now has branches in North America (New York and California), British Honduras and the Bahamas, as well as in England, but Jamaica, with something over fifty congregations, remains its stronghold.

The City Mission in London has close contacts with its two bishops in the United States, both of whom have visited England, one for a period of more than a year. But in this case there is no question of the bishops' exercising surveillance on behalf of an American headquarters, as the headquarters is in Jamaica. Nor are English congregations helped financially by the American ones; if anything the reverse is true: money has been collected in England to defray the bishops' travelling expenses.

The City Mission is the only one of the sects under discussion to have female bishops.[6] The prominence of women in positions of authority is the result of their prominence in the early evangelistic work of the Salvation Army in Jamaica.[7] The refusal of other sects to have female bishops derives from the rather patriarchal nature of

[6] It is not a City Mission doctrine that only women should be bishops. When Mary Coore was named by Raglan Phillips as his successor it was natural that she should choose her closest associates, to take charge of new overseas congregations. These happened to be women.

[7] All but one of the Jesus Name sects are vehemently opposed to women preaching

society in the Deep South of the United States at the turn of the century. As Jamaican society is anything but patriarchal it is unlikely that this prejudice is very deep seated among Jamaicans. Leaders (often themselves bishops) of other sects in England freely refer to the City Mission bishops as 'bishop' and always address them by this title. Having female bishops is no bar to co-operation with other sects, indeed some Church of God congregations co-operate more often and more closely with the City Mission than they do with one another. Nevertheless, all other sects condemn this City Mission usage as unscriptural and, as we shall see in Chapter V, it can provide excellent biblical justification for fission.

3. *Sect Membership and Migration*

Practically all members of the Pentecostal sects to be discussed later are from Jamaica. As is shown in Table 3, about 66 per cent of

TABLE 3
Island Derivation of Migrants

Island	Number	Percentage
Jamaica	57,000	66
British Guiana	2,350	6
Barbados	7,200	8
Trinidad	4,400	5
Windward Islands	8,100	9
Leeward Islands	8,100	9
Total	87,150	100

all West Indian migrants come from Jamaica and no more than 9 per cent from any other Caribbean island or territory.

There are no towns in England in which Jamaicans are not in the

or holding the office of bishop; the other Churches of God object as well, but less vehemently:
'God has never called and sent a woman to preach the gospel and never will. Every woman that says God called her to preach the gospel is lying on God' . . . and of women bishops: 'Some women are so deceived of the devil they call themselves bishops. The Bible says: "This is a true saying, If a MAN desires the office of a bishop HE [Not She] desireth a good work . . ." Therefore every woman preacher is lost and on her way to destruction because she is deceived of the devil and lied on God.' Of course, even in those sects that condemn women preachers most violently, women play a very active part. This is possible because of the technical distinction between testifying and preaching; the Bible does not say that women may not testify, and therefore their participation is always called testimony.

majority, and the big populations of Barbadians in Reading and St. Lucians in Slough, for example, are matched by equally large Jamaican populations. It is likely that immigrants from other islands are reluctant to join sects because they are dominated by Jamaicans. Very few towns have a population from any Caribbean territory other than Jamaica large enough to support a sect. Barbadians in Reading broke away from a Jamaican-dominated sect to start their own, but in the two years (1961–3) during which I have followed its fortunes it has had not more than five members, so this experiment has hardly proved successful.

Jamaicans comprise so overwhelming a majority of sect members that the influence of immigrants from other islands can be safely disregarded. Followers of a sect from islands other than Jamaica are usually peripheral members of it; it is very unusual to find non-Jamaicans among the nuclear members to be discussed in Chapter VIII. This is the general picture over a period of time; during the three years of this study some sect congregations did attract fairly large followings from islands other than Jamaica, but these people did not stay long. My discussions with sect leaders suggest that this pattern has been common at least since the mid fifties; some of them claimed to have had a non-Jamaican following in the past although they have practically no non-Jamaican following today.

I have found it very difficult to determine whether West Indian Pentecostals in this country were, before emigrating, members of the same sect as that they are attached to here. (Here I use 'member' in the strict sense, to mean one who has been formally accepted into the church, who has had 'the hand of fellowship' extended to him.) This difficulty is due very largely to the use (in this country and the West Indies though not the United States) of the name 'Church of God' for so many quite different and separate organisations. This was touched on in Chapter II, where it was also seen that West Indians use 'Church of God' as part of a sect title only for Father, Son, and Holy Ghost sects; for convenience it is so used here.

City Mission members who come to this country seem to remain loyal to their original sect, but the City Mission, differing as it does from others in important ritual as well as its system of leadership, etc., is not characteristic: its members will find nowhere else the satisfaction of familiar proceedings they are looking for. Jesus Name and Church of God groups, on the other hand, share very similar rituals and organisational structure, and it seems that members derive identical satisfactions from belonging to either group. Jesus Name members who had at home belonged to a Church of God sect, which baptised in the name of Father, Son, and Holy Ghost, would have to undergo another baptismal ceremony, and the frequency with which Jesus Name groups here hold baptisms suggests that a high proportion (probably a quarter to a half) of their members are converts of this sort. Many members and at least one leader of a Jesus Name sect admit to having been converted to the Jesus Name doctrine since coming to England.

It seems likely that, in the Church of God groups, a similar proportion of members were, in the West Indies, members of different sects from those they now belong to, though they probably came from some sort of Church of God sect. As all Church of God sects perform the same ritual and hold almost identical doctrinal views, it does not matter to the ordinary migrant which one he joins; to him, all are acceptable alternatives and his choice is largely a matter of chance, depending on which congregation he comes to hear of first or which meets closest to where he lives. This does not mean that he treats his association with a congregation lightly; his loyalty develops quickly in an atmosphere of shared ritual and intimate social contact.

It is not easy to get saints to discuss their choice of a church on arrival in England in other than religious terms. They say they were 'led' by God to join a particular congregation, and consider this a sufficient explanation. However, on many occasions I have been asked by migrants attending a congregation service for the first time which church it was they were attending. When I asked the name of the church they attended in Jamaica they almost invariably replied 'Church of God' without indicating which.[8] Some of these people later became members of the congregation in which I met them. The ordinary migrant, then, does not look about for a congregation of the particular Church of God with which he was associated in his home island, but tends to join the first Church of God congregation he hears of, if, of course, he joins one at all.[9]

---

[8] In some of these cases failure to name a specific Church of God was due to there being only one in the rural district the migrant came from. Many migrants can become aware of the multiplicity of Churches of God only after living in an English city.

[9] There are a few intensely religious people who wander from congregation to congregation without joining any of them. These differ from the ordinary person, discussed in Chapter VIII, who is not a member of any congregation but may very intermittently attend the meetings of several, in that they are preoccupied with religion to about the same degree as nuclear congregation members. They deserve mention as aberrants in a system of tightly organised congregations, but are numerically unimportant; I have met only five.

This applies to the ordinary migrant who becomes an ordinary member of a sect, but less certainly to those who become nuclear members. Because they are more aware of and more interested in the slight doctrinal differences between sect and sect they are more selective than ordinary members, more inclined to seek a sect congregation preaching the exact doctrine they have been used to in Jamaica. If there is no sect in the area in which they settle which does this, then they are likely to start one of their own rather than compromise. On the other hand, because they are more interested in religion they are more likely to be converted from one doctrinal point of view to another. An estimated quarter of the nuclear members of sect congregations have at some time in their lives been members of other sects.

Even though migrants who were members of a particular sect in Jamaica do not necessarily join the same one in England they are very likely to join some sect. About four-fifths of the members of the four sect congregations I was able to study in detail had been at least associated with Pentecostal churches in the West Indies before coming to England. Less detailed analysis of other sect congregations suggests that this is a general pattern.

As I shall suggest in later chapters, those who become members of sects in England are a small proportion of those who were in some way associated with Pentecostal sects in the West Indies; these people are used to a Pentecostal form of worship, and are therefore potential members. It appears that continuity is an important factor in the development of sects in England; West Indian migrants have transplanted a familiar pattern of group organisation, and to some extent the development of sects amounts to a re-creation of the Caribbean in England.

But why should these groups be transplanted when others are not? This is accounted for by their special characteristics. Sect congregations are characteristically recruited by voluntary association; members join them as adults or sub-adults. West Indian migration to England has been a migration of individuals, not of kin groups. Even where kin groups have re-formed in England, members have migrated separately. Where a family has re-formed it has usually taken many years to do so, and the process has been impeded by the hope of so many migrants of returning home after a few years in England; men have been deterred from sending for their wives and families because they expect separation to be of short duration. Groups recruiting by voluntary association are the only ones that could emerge in an immigrant population composed of isolated individuals. Religious groups are not the only associations of this type that have emerged; their rise has been accompanied by an increase in the number of West Indian social clubs.

IV

THE DYNAMICS OF SECT FORMATION

1. *The Growth of Congregations*

Most Pentecostal West Indians when asked why they came to England answer in religious terms. They say that they were called to do God's work in foreign lands. He who leaves his own country must perforce be a missionary, and thus Pentecostal migrants see themselves. Some say that at home in Jamaica they heard that the English had fallen away from God and were led to undertake their reconversion; that they felt 'a burden for the souls' of their countrymen in England, and for those of the Godless English. I doubt whether many working-class West Indians know much about the practice of religion in England before they arrive here; most I have spoken to say that they always understood that England was a 'great Christian country' and they are surprised to discover how few English people attend church. It is possible, however, that the West Indian Pentecostal is better informed than the average migrant on this subject, especially if he has read letters from Pentecostals already settled in England, or has met members who have returned home. Letters certainly contain references to religious matters,[1] and the experiences of returned Pentecostals must feature in their testimonies at church services. Of recent years successful religious leaders have taken to going home for extended holidays during which they take a prominent part in the religious life of their native communities, and sometimes also go on preaching tours.

It is possible, then, that religious motives do play some part in the West Indian Pentecostal's decision to come to England, but they also provide a handy rationalisation for economic ones. Strictly speaking truly fervent Christians should not have economic motives, which are 'of this world', so they are not always ready to admit them. Nevertheless nearly all Pentecostals with whom I have discussed this agreed, when pressed, that they came in search of work and prosperity just as non-Pentecostal West Indians do, and also like them, they look forward to returning one day to the West Indies.

---

[1] Some Pentecostal leaders model even their private correspondence on the Epistles of St. Paul; thus letter-writing is a sect ritual up to a point, and letters are composed of ritual phrases. Some I have received convey no information at all.

In all respects except their devotion to religion, Pentecostals, or 'saints', as they call themselves, are typical of the West Indian population in England; most are unskilled workers, a few are skilled workers, fewer still hold white-collar jobs. Like other West Indians the saint often finds himself unable to find employment in the trade he learned in the Caribbean, either because his trade qualifications are not recognised by English unions and employers or because his skills are little in demand in England; consequently many are doing work less skilled than that they did in Jamaica.

The educational level of saints is also typical of working-class migrants as a whole. All but two of those I have come to know are literate, though some clearly do not read very easily. In one respect they are better educated than other migrants; they all have a very detailed knowledge of the Bible and their speech is enriched by biblical vocabulary and allusion.

The aspiring religious leader must find himself followers from among the West Indians he knows. These may be drawn from his place of work, from the house in which he lives, or from among the members of another already established sect congregation whose services he attends. It is not unlikely that he will get a job where other Pentecostal West Indians work, as saints tend to recommend one another. He is also likely to live in a house occupied by other saints as they prefer to let rooms to one another. And at a meeting, particularly a large meeting, of any other West Indian sect he is likely to find people who are not very firmly attached to it, and who may be willing to join him.

Not all congregation leaders start in this way. Some of them are initially more or less contented members of someone else's congregation and only lead a breakaway movement and establish a new congregation when dissensions arise within it.[2]

Whatever the origin of the group it usually commences meeting in the rented room in which one of the members (most likely the leader) lives. If membership increases it may try to rent a larger room or hall and undertake proselytising campaigns to bring itself to the attention of other West Indians in the neighbourhood.

If any members have children, a Sunday School is organised and people in the neighbourhood, whether they are members or not, are asked to send their children to it. West Indians who are not members of it are nevertheless likely to feel that religious training will be good

[2] The processes of fission and fusion will be discussed more fully in Chapter V.

for their children and send them along.[3] The offices of Deacon, Elder, Treasurer, sometimes Secretary, Sunday School teacher, Youth Leader and Evangelist are distributed among members so that as many as possible of them can be made to feel that they are important in the life of the nascent church. Where there are more traditional offices than members, a member is given more than one office. This doling out of offices is often performed regardless of the suitability of members for the offices given to them. A woman who read only with the greatest difficulty was appointed Sunday School Teacher in one London congregation. Occasionally, young men in their twenties are appointed Elders, though this is likely to be criticised on the grounds that the Bible implies that only married men with families should be Elders. At the only two inaugural meetings of sect congregations I was able to attend, members were obviously delighted at being given office in the church.

The greatest problem the new congregation has to face is finding somewhere to meet at a rent it can afford. A large well-established congregation, especially one whose members pay tithes, can afford to to pay £5 or £6 rent for each service, but a new small one is unlikely to be able to afford more than a pound or so. For this reason small congregations are constantly seeking more advantageous terms and often change their places of meeting.[4] This makes them difficult to find, thus reducing their chances of recruiting new members.

Of the sect congregations in London more than half meet in halls or rooms attached to halls rented from English Protestant churches. The rest rent rooms from schools, political parties, co-operative societies, local authorities and, in one case, the University of London. In 1962, five congregations met in the basements of West Indian-owned private houses in which dividing walls had been removed to give a space large enough to seat up to fifty people.

This last arrangement has the advantage that the room is used only as a church and can be equipped like one, but the disadvantage that

---

[3] Some sects place great emphasis on their Sunday Schools and sometimes native English as well as West Indian parents can be persuaded to send their (young) children to it. This tendency is more strongly marked in the Midlands than in London; the London congregations of the City Mission have no white children attending their Sunday School, whereas about half the sixteen children attending the Birmingham congregation's Sunday School are white. The Church of God of Prophecy in Birmingham has had remarkable success in this direction, though I am sceptical of one congregation's claim to a nearly all-white Sunday School with seventy enrolled members.

[4] One London congregation has changed its meeting place four times in the last two years.

the building does not look like a church from the outside. Usually such basement churches have no door opening directly onto the street and must be entered through the house, so that strangers have difficulty in finding their way in. A notice-board on the street does not appear to make much difference. Taken all in all, this solution to the accommodation problem is an unsatisfactory one and the congregations of many basement churches consist of the occupants of the house only; it becomes little more than a private chapel.

Besides their cost, rented halls have the disadvantage that the owners usually stipulate that meetings must not continue beyond about nine o'clock in the evening. Were it not for this many of them would continue into the early hours of the morning, as it is considered wrong to restrict the workings of 'the Spirit' by man-made rules.[5]

Owners of halls are always sensitive to the protests of local non-West Indian residents against the noise of Pentecostal services[6] and some are reluctant to let halls to West Indians at all because of the noise they are reputed to make. Some such protests are quite justified: two hundred people shouting 'Praise the Lord' all at once can be quite deafening; but the average congregation is much smaller than this and not nearly so noisy. Indeed, some services cannot be heard from the street. Protests have been made against small congregations that could not have been very noisy, which suggests that in some cases white neighbours are protesting against the neighbourhood acquiring a West Indian flavour from the presence of a West Indian sect, rather than against the noise they make. This is particularly likely to happen when the hall is some distance from where sect members live and not in an area of dense West Indian settlement. Because a place to meet is hard to find, congregation leaders range far afield in search of one.

In addition to these difficulties, if a congregation rents a hall that is used for other purposes as well, it can seldom put up notices, display tracts or leave hymn-books and musical instruments there, so all the paraphernalia of sect worship must be carried back and forth between the hall and the homes of members.

For these reasons nearly all sects in England aspire to buy their own hall one day. Apart from the convenience of being able to hold services whenever and for as long as 'the Spirit leads', owning pre-

---

[5] I have attended services that, starting at ten in the morning, have continued until eleven o'clock at night; but two to three hours is the normal length.

[6] I have recorded seven such protests during the last two years. It is likely that nearly all congregations are the subjects of protests at some stage in their history.

mises is essential if the congregation is ever to be completely independent of the established Protestant denominations. At present all of them depend on being able to borrow a Baptist or English Pentecostal church with a tank for total immersion baptism.[7] Baptismal ceremonies are essential to the proper induction of new members, as all these sects believe that only those who have been baptised can enter heaven. Most sects borrow a Baptist church; I know of only one instance of the Elim Church having lent premises to a West Indian sect for the performance of a baptism ceremony.

It is also essential for a sect congregation to own a building if it is to perform its own marriage ceremonies. In England, a building is licensed at a fee of £2 per annum for the performance of marriage ceremonies and it is generally only church buildings that are licensed. In addition an 'authorised person' (the minister or official of the building concerned) must be present at the ceremony. There appears to be no reason why this person should not be the congregation leader, if the congregation owned a licensed building. This means that the marriage rites of members must usually be performed by a clergyman of one of the recognised churches; I have recorded no case of a clergyman being willing to lend his church unless he performs the rite. Until quite recently this was not a serious problem, there being few West Indian women in England, and therefore few marriages. But in the last two years a much higher proportion of the immigrants have been women and the number of marriages among sect members has increased. Sect leaders find their dependence on the established churches frustrating; it diminishes their prestige as religious leaders.

2. *Sect Building and Relations between Sects*

When a leader has established a congregation he may be approached by the leader of one of the larger sects asking him to bring his 'work' under its aegis. Various inducements are offered, principal among which is a title, usually that of 'overseer'[8] for a particular area of England. For example a sect leader in Birmingham may offer to

---

[7] One enterprising West Indian congregation is making use of a public swimming-pool in East London (1963). None of the West Indian sects in England have baptised in the open air, in rivers or the sea, but some English Pentecostal sects have done so in the past. The Jehovah's Witnesses have done so more recently.

[8] In large sects the leader in England is usually called 'bishop'. He may also be called 'general overseer', 'overseer for Great Britain' or some such title. There is nothing to prevent leaders of small sects calling themselves 'overseer' and some do; at present none of them call themselves 'bishop'.

appoint a congregation leader he wants to join him 'Overseer of London'.

A congregation leader does not always respond to a sect leader's invitation to join his movement. In 1962 a leader of the Pentecostal Churches of the World, a Jesus Name sect with headquarters in the Midlands, approached the young leader of the Church of the Living God, which at the time had two congregations, offering to appoint him 'Overseer' of Berkshire. But the offer was rejected on the grounds that the Pentecostal Churches of the World 'did not teach correct doctrine'. Normally the rejection of an overture for union must be justified by an actual or fancied difference in doctrine, as must sect fission.

If the new congregation does not join one of the large sect organisations its leader will try to build up a sect organisation of his own, extending his personal authority either by persuading other independent congregation leaders to bring their congregations into his organisation, or by developing new congregations from the residue of members left by his revival campaigns and appointing congregation leaders to run them for him. He may also attempt to detach members from other leaders to provide the nucleus of a congregation, and though, as we shall see, leaders are dependent on the goodwill and co-operation of other leaders they are wary of them. 'Sheep stealing' is an important aspect of inter-sect relations.

Sect fission does not necessarily result in a permanently independent sect. Sometimes the breakaway leader leads his congregation out of one sect organisation into another competing one. This happened with two congregations of the Church of God in Christ in 1957 and 1959. The leader of the 1957 breakaway called his sect the 'All Nations Church of God'. It existed independently for about a year and then became a constituent congregation of the New Testament Church of God. The 1959 breakaway, calling itself the Grace and Truth Association, joined the New Testament Church of God in early 1960 after only a few months of independent operation. In this way the New Testament Church of God, until then a sect operating mainly in the Midlands,[9] gained a foothold in London with two numerous, well-led congregations. Since then it has become almost as influential in London as it is in the Midlands.

All these processes have played their part in the building of the large sect organisations in England. Sometimes the three processes are quite distinct, but more often they overlap. The residue after a

[9] Because the person who started the first congregation happened to live in Wolverhampton.

revival campaign usually includes people who were members of other sect congregations until the revival took place.

The history of the Church of the Living God, which has grown very rapidly, illustrates all three processes of sect formation. Its first congregation in Reading in 1962 was composed partly of people lured away from another independent sect congregation, the Victorious Church of God, and partly of the residue left by a revival campaign. Its second congregation in East London was composed entirely of converts of a revival campaign. In early 1962 the leader persuaded a hitherto independent congregation in Slough to join him and towards the end of 1962 established a fourth congregation after a rally in Birmingham.

The rapid growth of this sect is typical of sect organisations generally;[10] since commencing operations in England some of them have added congregations at the rate of about one a year.

Table 4 illustrates the development of the Church of God of Prophecy in the Birmingham area between 1957 and 1961. Membership figures are those for April 1961.

TABLE 4

The Development of the Church of God of Prophecy

Congregation	A	B	C	D	E	F
Date Established	1957	1958	1959	1960	1960	1961
Number of Members	80–90	40	20	20	20	15

A sect organisation built by these processes is not necessarily stable thereafter; as we have seen, two congregations broke away from the Church of God in Christ in the late 1950's. There is always a certain tension between the centralised sect organisation and its constituent assemblies. But providing tension does not lead to fission it has a definite integrative function. Sect congregations compete in holiness, in proselytisation and in the formation of daughter-congregations as well as in the lavishness with which they entertain one another at conventions and rallies.

Nevertheless it is the congregation rather than the sect which benefits from this increased solidarity; despite the sect leader's boasts

---

[10] Its collapse at the end of 1963 was every bit as spectacular. The Reading and Slough congregations fell away and the North London one disintegrated to the point at which only three people attended a meeting at Easter 1964. This congregation has now ceased meeting and the leader is engaged in trying to build a new congregation from a new body of converts.

of his world-wide affiliations and the number of congregations recognising his authority, the congregation is by far the more important group.

If, as is usually the case with the larger sect, congregations are geographically dispersed, there are no occasions on which it meets together as a group. The largest group ever meeting together comprises a cluster of congregations in the same big city or closely neighbouring towns.[11] In its regular activities the congregation of one of the large sects has as much to do with congregations of other sects in the same locality as it has with other, more distant, congregations of the sect it belongs to.

Although each sect considers itself to be ideologically distinct[12] and the sole possessor of the key to heaven, there is a great deal of co-operation and co-activity among them. Practically never does a sect congregation hold a big meeting without inviting members of some other sects and without their attending. On one occasion I counted representatives of five separate sects on the platform at a big City Mission meeting, though the average would be about three. Indeed no big meeting, rally or convention can take place without the co-operation of other sects. The significance of the occasion is much reduced if there are not many important people on the platform. The presence of so many leaders impresses the rank and file with the importance of their congregation.

In summer invitations are more frequent than in winter. During the summer of 1962 hardly a week went by without some City Mission members attending the meeting of another sect. When these meetings were held at the same time as regular City Mission meetings a few City Mission representatives attended. When they did not clash with City Mission meetings up to half of the City Mission congregation would attend. In the winter of 1962 City Mission members attended meetings of other sects at about monthly intervals.

Not every sect congregation co-operates with every other operating in the same town or district. Sometimes personal antipathies between

---

[11] Congregations from London, Reading and Slough have held services in common, as have congregations from Birmingham, Wolverhampton and Walsall. Occasionally the London congregation of the City Mission travels to Birmingham to have 'fellowship' with the Birmingham one, but on only one occasion have more than eight London members made the trip.

[12] One preacher addressed his congregation of eight people as follows: 'Brethren, I don't want you to think that we are the only ones with a full understanding of the Gospel message, there is another church that has it as well.' The other church had ten members.

congregation leaders prevent it. And Father, Son and Holy Ghost congregations practically never co-operate with Jesus Name ones.[13]

Thus, although the various sects are in competition (often quite open competition) they are nevertheless interdependent. Not only does the currency of conflicting doctrines make members more aware of those characteristic of their own sect, but they depend on the co-operation of other sects whenever their enthusiasm and solidarity need buttressing by a large, spectacular meeting.

Only West Indian sects participate in this play of conflict and co-operation. As if by common agreement, other religious groups, including, significantly, the English Pentecostal ones, are excluded. A sect leader neither pirates the members of English Pentecostal churches nor invites their leaders to his meetings.[14] Any West Indian congregation leader knows of all the others in the same city, and is personally acquainted with half or two thirds of them. Leaders and members alike feel that the West Indian sects as a group represent a distinct, separate branch of Christianity in England, in spite of their diversity in doctrine and the fact that some of them are doctrinally closer to English Pentecostal churches than they are to each other.

In Table 5 I have listed the sects occurring in England together with the approximate number of congregations in each. This gives the situation in mid-1962, but because congregations are constantly dying and coming into being, severing links with sect organisations and forming new ones, it is not exhaustive. The total of seventy-seven congregations is certainly a conservative one since I must have failed to record some of them in towns I was unable to visit very often. Many sect leaders mentioned new congregations, not counted here, that were in the process of starting when I last surveyed them. It is also likely that many new, independent congregations have started since I made this detailed survey in 1962, without my hearing about them. The total number now is likely to be well over a hundred.

---

[13] The exception is the Pentecostal Evangelistic Fellowship, a group which baptises in the name of the Trinity.

[14] This is generally true but I have recorded exceptions. The Church of the Living God has, on occasion, invited white Pentecostals from Wales to attend its meetings. For a while in 1961 an independent white Pentecostal group with some West Indian members was 'in fellowship' with its Reading congregation, but this association lasted only a few months, and ended with the leaders quarrelling bitterly. On one occasion the Church of God in Christ in Luton held a service together with the local Elim Church.

TABLE 5

Sects in England and the Numbers of their Congregations

Sect	Number of Congregations
Church of God in Christ	7
Church of God of Prophecy	16
New Testament Church of God	23
Church of the Lord Jesus Christ of the Apostolic Faith	2
Pentecostal Churches of the World*	4
New Covenant Church of God	2
International Evangelistic Fellowship	2
City Mission	3
Victorious Church of God	1
Church of the Living God	3
Anglo-West Indian Assembly	1
Independent Church of God (four separate sects)	10
Independent Jesus Name (three separate sects)	3
Total	77

* I was unable to contact the leader of this group and have probably underestimated its importance. It may have three times as many congregations. Some confusion is also caused by this sect often calling itself Church of God in Christ Jesus (apostolic). I have also several times heard it called simply 'Church of God in Christ', which obviously causes it to be confused with the first group listed here.

In Table 6 the English towns in which there were sects in 1962 are listed with the sects occurring in them. This is most accurate for London and towns close to London and in the Midlands, and least accurate for those distant from London that I was able to visit less often.

Diagram II gives the genealogical relationships among the sects in England in 1962, their fissions and unions. This equally is not exhaustive, because in compiling it I was dependent on the memories of informants for splits and unions before 1960. It is not altogether satisfactory to represent sect development genealogically; the diagram is a simplification. It does not show sect congregations now dead.

3. *The Death of Congregations*

Despite the overall success of the West Indian Pentecostal sects, not every congregation is successful. Some never manage to gather a

TABLE 6

Sects Occurring in English Towns and Number of Congregations

Town	Independent Jesus Name	Independent Church of God	Church of the Living God	Victorious Church of God	City Mission	International Evangelistic Fellowship	New Covenant Church of God	Pentecostal Churches of the World	Church of the Lord Jesus Christ of the Apostolic Faith	Church of God in Christ	Church of God of Prophecy	New Testament Church of God
Bedford											1	
Birmingham, including Walsall and Wolverhampton					2	1			4	1	7	6
Bristol											1	
Coventry	1											1
Derby											1	
Dudley												1
Gloucester												1
Huddersfield	1	1										
Leeds												1
Liverpool	1											1
Greater London	3	8	1		2	1	2	2	2	5	2	9
Luton		1								1		
Manchester	1											1
Northampton												1
Nottingham											1	1
Oxford										1		
Reading		1	1	1								
Rugby												1
Sheffield											1	1
Slough	1									1		

Diagram II. Sect Development in England

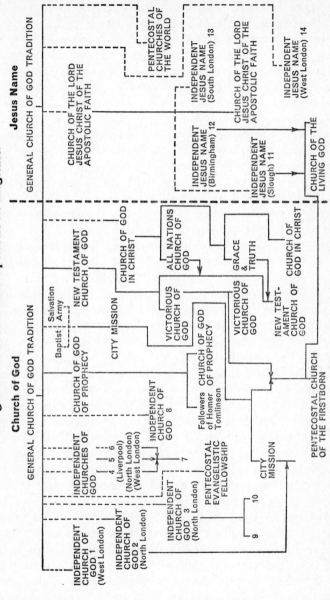

Church of God   **Jesus Name**

GENERAL CHURCH OF GOD TRADITION

GENERAL CHURCH OF GOD TRADITION

PENTECOSTAL CHURCHES OF THE WORLD

CHURCH OF THE LORD JESUS CHRIST OF THE APOSTOLIC FAITH

INDEPENDENT JESUS NAME (South London) 13

CHURCH OF THE LORD JESUS CHRIST OF THE APOSTOLIC FAITH

INDEPENDENT JESUS NAME (West London) 14

INDEPENDENT JESUS NAME (Birmingham) 12

INDEPENDENT JESUS NAME (Slough) 11

CHURCH OF THE LIVING GOD

Baptist   Salvation Army

NEW TESTAMENT CHURCH OF GOD

CHURCH OF GOD IN CHRIST

ALL NATIONS CHURCH OF GOD

CITY MISSION

CHURCH OF GOD OF PROPHECY

VICTORIOUS CHURCH OF GOD

GRACE & TRUTH

VICTORIOUS CHURCH OF GOD

CHURCH OF GOD IN CHRIST

NEW TEST- AMENT CHURCH OF GOD

Followers of Homer Tomlinson CHURCH OF GOD OF PROPHECY

INDEPENDENT CHURCHES OF GOD

4   5   6

(Liverpool) (North London) (West London)

INDEPENDENT CHURCH OF GOD 8

7

PENTECOSTAL EVANGELISTIC FELLOWSHIP

PENTECOSTAL CHURCH OF THE FIRSTBORN

INDEPENDENT CHURCH OF GOD 1 (West London)

INDEPENDENT CHURCH OF GOD 2 (North London)

INDEPENDENT CHURCH OF GOD 3 (North London)

CITY MISSION

9   10

congregation, others wither after an initial period of success, and still others are killed by a hard English winter.

The rapidity with which sects appear and decline makes it difficult to say just what proportion of those that start fail to establish themselves permanently, but the impression I have received during the period of my study has been of a steady increase in the number of those operating. This increase may be due to the rising proportion of women among the immigrants over the last two years; a higher proportion of congregations may have failed in the 1950's before women started to arrive in large numbers. Women are more firmly attached to Pentecostal patterns of worship than are men.

Those sects that fail to gather a congregation usually do so because the West Indian population in the district in which services are arranged is not very dense. A congregation in Hampstead, close to Kilburn, provides a particularly good example of this. Very few working-class West Indians live in the area. In 1962 it numbered only the leader, his wife and two or three people living in the same building. Often no service was held for months on end.

There appears to be an absolute minimum population a district or town must have before it can support a sect congregation. This is somewhere between three and five hundred. Since about 1956 unsuccessful attempts had been made to establish a congregation in Oxford. This was finally achieved in 1962 when the West Indian population increased somewhat. The presence of one sect congregation stimulates the development of others so that there are few towns with only one; if there are any at all there tend to be two or three. This is partly because the original group includes people who in the West Indies were members of several different sects; they are initially willing to bury their differences, but they ultimately split into separate congregations. It is also because leaders in other cities, hearing that a congregation is operating, realise the potentialities of a new field and start competing congregations of their own.

Sometimes a congregation disappears because the leader loses interest or finds himself unable to cope with the practical problems of running it. This happened with a congregation in Harlesden in 1961 which the leader tried to persuade the City Mission to take over and run as a branch of their main work in the Holloway-Stoke Newington area. More rarely a congregation disintegrates when the leader returns to the West Indies or moves to another town.

A congregation may also disappear due to disagreement among its members. Characteristically this results in a split; two congregations meet where one met before. But if the original congregation is very small it may cease meeting entirely. Members lose interest and cease attending Pentecostal services at all, or transfer their allegiance to other congregations if there are any within easy reach.

A congregation may disintegrate if members come to believe the leader to have been guilty of breaking taboos, usually those on extra-marital sexual intercourse. They refuse to follow him any longer and transfer their allegiance elsewhere. The bare suggestion of 'sin' of this kind on the part of a leader may be enough to detach his congregation from him though I have heard of only one congregation disintegrating for this reason. 'Sin' impairs his religious 'mana'[15] and one who is addicted to it cannot hope to maintain close touch with the Holy Ghost, nor can he assist his congregation to do so. Other leaders are quick to dissociate themselves from one suspected of 'sin'. I quote from a circular letter of a London sect: '. . . there is an apostolic assembly somewhere in Birmingham or the Midlands that a minister have been found guilty of some terrible sin and it is widely rumoured that this minister is one of my officers and still leading one of my assembly. This man and his assembly have nothing to do with me or the Church of —— . . .'

West Indians' attendance at religious services is directly dependent on the weather and unless a congregation is very firmly established it is likely to be killed by a hard winter. Most migrants adjust to the cold and damp of England by staying indoors as much as they possibly can. One elderly woman told me of her first experience of a London fog. Convinced that the end of the world had come and that the advent of Christ was imminent, she spent the whole day praying for deliverance in her room.

Even very well established congregations suffer severely in the winter. On New Year's Day 1962 only one saint arrived for a scheduled service in the City Mission, and during the phenomenally severe cold spell of 1962–3 religious activity in public halls ceased entirely, though the group continued to meet in a private house. Table 7 indicates the manner in which attendance declines in the winter. In this table I have excluded the earlier part of 1961 as the presence of three bishops caused congregations to be unusually large: up to six hundred and averaging about one hundred. I have also excluded

---

[15] I do not feel the use of this term to be inappropriate in the discussion of Pentecostal sects. See Luke viii, 46: 'And Jesus said, Somebody hath touched me: for I perceive that virtue is gone out of me.' The 'gifts of the Holy Spirit' can be reasonably thought of as 'mana'.

TABLE 7

Average Attendance at City Mission Services
August 1961 *to July* 1962

Month	Average Number Attending Services
August	33
October	15
November	15
December	8
January	13
February	12
March	10
April	17
May	26
June	31
July	35

special meetings such as rallies and conventions which are better attended than the average meeting.

Sickness among members also causes attendances to fall off in winter, and there is a marked increase in requests for prayers for sick relatives. I have the impression that there is more sickness in the West Indian community during winter than in the population as a whole. This may be partly due to lack of adaptation to a cold climate, but the West Indian is generally less well nourished and well housed than English people; his living conditions are crowded and lacking in comfort. And to the West Indian coughs and colds are real illnesses, sufficient to keep him indoors if not in bed.

Most sect congregations recover their membership when the spring comes, but a few of the weaker ones do not start up again. To my knowledge three London congregations were killed by the unusually hard winter of 1962–3.

V

FISSION AND DISPUTE

1. *Types of Fission*

WEST INDIAN Pentecostal sects in England are very subject to fission, as earlier discussion has indicated. In this chapter I shall describe the processes of fission in greater detail.

To facilitate discussion I distinguish two types of fission: sect fission and congregation fission. In the first, a congregation (very rarely more than one) of a sect composed of several congregations breaks away and declares itself independent. In the second, a congregation, which may be one in a multi-congregational sect or a one-congregation sect, splits to form two separate congregations. If the parent congregation was a member of a wider sect organisation, then one part after the split remains loyal to it while the other part starts operation as an independent, one-congregation sect. It may remain independent or it may join another multi-congregational sect later on.

As we have seen, continuity and the solidarity of Christian fellowship are valued, whereas causing 'dissension among the saints' is condemned as ungodly. Therefore when a split occurs those of both factions claim to represent the original church. A leader seldom admits to having led a breakaway movement, to having seceded; he generally claims to have been seceded from. If the dividing congregation belongs to a multi-congregational sect then the sect leader is likely to settle the issue, and the faction he supports will be accepted as the parent body by other member congregations of the sect and later by congregations outside the sect. But where the dividing congregation is an independent one there is no possibility of the question being settled by an outside authority, and therefore both factions claim to be the original, parent body. Often they both use the name of the parent congregation, regardless of the confusion this causes among other Christians and in the West Indian population generally. Occasionally one faction retains the old name and one takes a new name, and very rarely both factions assume new names.

Congregation fission and sect fission are not always distinct. In sect fission a few members may refuse to follow the breakaway

leader, out of loyalty to the sect leader, who may use them as the
nucleus around which he tries to organise a new congregation to
replace the one he has lost. If there seems little likelihood of starting
a new congregation to replace the lost one, then the remnant faithful
to the sect leader is absorbed into another congregation of the sect.
In all the cases of sect fission I recorded, the breakaway was led by
the congregation leader.

Fission can be said to have occurred only when a new religious
group, worshipping together as a congregation, emerges. I am not
describing as fission the withdrawal or 'disfellowshipment' (excommunication) of one member, though once again the distinction is
not always clear-cut. An attempt to lead a breakaway movement may
prove unsuccessful, those who initially followed the breakaway
ultimately drifting back into the parent congregation, leaving the
leader of the breakaway with no followers. Again, one who has withdrawn or been 'disfellowshipped' may succeed in building up a congregation by proselytising among West Indians who hitherto belonged
to no sect congregation or by luring away members from other sect
congregations. In such a case the continuity between the new congregation and the parent one is less obvious, and the distinction
between fission of the congregation and withdrawal or disfellowshipment of a member less clear-cut.

2. *Disfellowshipment*

A member's refusal to accept the congregation leader's ruling, or
consistent opposition to him, may be countered by excommunication
(called 'disfellowshipment'). Generally a leader is loth to disfellowship an insubordinate 'saint', as by doing so he is losing a member and
giving him to some other competing congregation. But on the other
hand he may feel that it is better to lose a member than risk having
him lead others out of the church. Disfellowshipment for insubordination alone is rather unusual; it is more usual for the leader to bring
other charges as well, very often those of breaking sexual taboos.

The split from the Church of the Living God in Reading to form
the Pentecostal Church of the First Born came about in just this way.
A member challenged the authority of the leader, who retaliated by
accusing him of having divorced one wife and married another, which
is of course not permissible in these sects. Both contestants then
talked with tongues at the same time, one against the other, each
trying to demonstrate to the congregation that he was the more holy,
that God was on his side. The service (which I attended) ended

without either of them giving ground, despite efforts by other members to act as 'peacemakers' and heal the breach. The following week I heard that the member had been disfellowshipped, and a month later that he was running an independent congregation.

No charges other than insubordination were levelled against a rebellious deacon of the Church of the Living God congregation in East London in 1962. This time the leader composed a formal statement of disfellowshipment which he read at services. Although the rebel was not present the leader felt it necessary to talk in tongues more than he normally did, to impress on the congregation that he was acting according to the will of God. A few weeks later the breach had been healed and the deacon accepted back into the congregation, but a second breach led to his final and this time permanent disfellowshipment. As far as I know he has not started a congregation of his own, nor did any of the Church of the Living God members follow him.

If a leader feels obliged to take the extreme action of disfellowshipping a member he must be able to carry the congregation with him. Talking with tongues is one way of doing this, of persuading members that his action is according to the will of God. But if the member to be disfellowshipped is present at the service he is likely to spoil the effect by talking with tongues himself. A better way of ensuring the congregation's support is to make it appear to be their decision rather than the leader's. The leader calls a meeting and persuades them to agree; some congregations even formally put it to the vote, but others feel that there is no biblical justification for such democratic procedure.

The Church of God in Christ tries members formally for suspected offences against the church and punishes them by 'suspension' (temporary) or 'disfellowshipment' (permanent). The New Testament Church of God has strict regulations governing the disfellowshipment of members and allows appeal against a congregation's decision; but as the courts of appeal are in the United States, this can have little relevance for the sect in England. The New Testament Church of God, like most of the larger sect organisations, does not recognise the right of constituent congregations to secede. If they do they must be disfellowshipped.

Some sect congregations are much less prone to disfellowship members than the Church of the Living God discussed above. I have heard of no case of formal disfellowshipment in the City Mission, whose leaders are content to let disgruntled members simply drift away to other sects without any formal severing of connections; perhaps this is partly because none of the leaders permanently resident in England feel confident of carrying the congregation with them in acts of disfellowshipment. But some other sects, with strong leadership, do not indulge in disfellowshipment either.

I have suggested that talking with tongues can be used by a congregation leader to elicit support in acts of disfellowshipment. It can also be used to gain support in less serious disputes. On one occasion a woman City Mission leader instructed the congregation to fast for two days,[1] saying that God had told her to do this in a revelation while she was praying. When she found out that few members had fasted she admonished them for lack of faith, and, to emphasise her point, engaged in the longest spate of speaking in tongues I have witnessed. Her authority had been questioned and doubt thrown on the genuineness of her revelation; therefore it was necessary to impress the congregation with her holiness.

A saint can establish or attempt to establish his holiness, and by implication the rightness of his point of view, by methods other than speaking in tongues. In an open breach that others know about he can gain support by announcing during a service that he forgives the person whom he considers to have wronged him. To be the first to announce forgiveness confers a clear advantage, and in those instances I have witnessed, the person forgiven felt obliged to announce forgiveness as well. Acts of forgiveness are greeted with jubilation by the congregation, which gives thanks to God for re-establishing the peace and goodwill appropriate to his church. But forgiveness does not imply that a disputant has given way or admitted being at fault; the hatchet is ritually buried for the time being, but may be dug up again later, and other members are well aware of this.

A quarrel in the City Mission between a woman leader and a young male member who felt that she was excessively domineering, although ritually buried by a rite of forgiveness, cropped up again two months later and finally resulted in the young man's withdrawal to join another congregation.

Disputes that have been ritually buried in this way can simmer for weeks or months, and though on the surface all appears to be well and the disputants publicly express love for one another, tension is evident. Sometimes this finds expression in ecstatic behaviour of

---

[1] Fasting means missing one (or perhaps two) meals a day, not total abstinence from food. It is a ritual act felt to be pleasing to God and therefore conducive to ecstatic experience.

more than usual extravagance, as if members were endeavouring to reassure themselves that all was well with the church while knowing that they were deluding themselves. The group counters a threat to its solidarity by performing a solidarity ritual with more than usual vigour; the Spirit does not fall in a divided church. If it does fall, rancour must have disappeared.

3. *Fission and Leadership*

Fission in a congregation generally divides both nuclear and ordinary members. Where one faction has a better claim to being the parent body, it will have the allegiance of the greater part of nuclear members.[2]

When the Church of the Living God split from the City Mission in 1961, those who followed it were all nuclear members. (See Table 8.) When the Church of the Living God itself split in 1962 to produce the Pentecostal Church of the First Born, about half the ordinary members followed each faction, as is shown in Table 9. The Church of the Living God had no chance whatever of claiming to be the parent body when it split from the City Mission and did not even attempt to do so, whereas the Pentecostal Church of the First Born had a fairly good chance of maintaining such a claim against the Church of the Living God.

TABLE 8

Fission, City Mission—Church of the Living God

Following City Mission		Following Church of the Living God	
Nuclear	*Ordinary*	*Nuclear*	*Ordinary*
18	21	4*	10

* One of these ultimately returned to the City Mission.

TABLE 9

Fission, Church of the Living God—Pentecostal Church of the First Born

Following Church of the Living God		Following Pentecostal Church of the First Born	
Nuclear	*Ordinary*	*Nuclear*	*Ordinary*
8	7	3	5

One other factor influences the allegiance of ordinary members when a congregation splits. If a minority of members come from

---

[2] 'Nuclear' members are those who participate intensively in congregation activities. For a discussion of this term see Chapter VIII.

islands other than Jamaica, they will all follow the same faction. Possibly island derivation is also a factor in the faction chosen by nuclear members.

In a congregation nucleus most or all of its members want to participate fully in ritual activities. All of them feel they are specially chosen to do God's work and are closely in touch with him.Convinced of their divine mission, they are impatient of any interference with it. The congregation leader is the most eminent nuclear member; few of them however would admit him to be more holy than they are: he is *primus inter pares*. His authority is accepted because, as was explained in Chapter IV, he started the congregation, but more important, because the New Testament describes churches as having leaders. To have them is the scriptural thing to do. God is pleased by the recognition of a leader by his saints, just as he is by their abjuring tobacco and fornication. Recognising a leader is as much a ritual act pleasing to God as it is an acceptance of the leader's ability. This is why a congregation can be led for a long time by someone who patently lacks any of the qualities commonly associated with a competent leader. The leader is generally the most competent of the nuclear members, but this is not always so.

Once a leader has been accepted it is difficult to challenge his authority. Leaders do not resign or retire,[3] so a member who aspires to the leadership cannot hope to supplant him while leaving the group intact. He must be willing to 'sow seeds of dissension among the children of God' and split the congregation, and he can contemplate this only if biblical authority can be found for doing so.

Although it is enjoined on the Christian to have Christian fellowship with others and to belong to a church, it is also enjoined on him to 'withdraw' himself from a church whose doctrine is false: 'Now we command you, brethren, in the name of our Lord Jesus Christ, that ye withdraw yourselves from every brother that walketh disorderly, and not after the tradition he received of us.' (II Thessalonians iii, 6.) This makes it particularly difficult to heal breaches. A leader sees himself as the heir of the Apostles, if not as a latter-day apostle, admonishing a wayward follower, whereas the follower can only regard the leader as one of the false prophets against whom Paul warned Titus: 'For there are many unruly and vain talkers and deceivers, specially they of the circumcision: Whose mouths must be stopped, who subvert whole houses, teaching things which they ought

---

[3] The only exception I recorded was in the Church of God in Christ. The leader (and founder in England) retired to the West Indies in 1963.

not, for filthy lucre's sake.' (Titus i, 10, 11.[4]) Both parties to the dispute see themselves in biblical roles which give them little room for manoeuvre and compromise. Because Paul distinguished himself by his intolerance they feel obliged to do so too, even when it is against their natural inclinations and better judgement.

The role of 'peacemaker', described as 'blessed' in the Sermon on the Mount (Matthew v, 9), would appear to offer a way out of this difficulty, but it is seen more as a ritual role than as a practical one. The 'peacemaker' does not genuinely arbitrate in a dispute, he either takes sides or appeals to the disputants to bury their differences and love one another. Often the peacemaker is more concerned with being thought 'blessed' than with the practical problems of arbitration, and the disputants may see him as one intent on gaining religious credit at their expense.

Although some leaders of breakaway movements may cold-bloodedly invent a doctrinal dispute after having decided to start a church of their own, I doubt whether this is very often the case. The situation is rather that personal ambition and general dissatisfaction go hand-in-hand with a searching of the scripture for an explanation for the dissatisfaction. The saint tries to discover in biblical terms why he feels restless and dissatisfied. His discovery that the congregation is not 'right with God' reinforces his perhaps unconscious desire to become a leader himself. The doctrinal issue most apt to this purpose and that most often used is 'church government'; it is claimed the congregation is not being run along strictly biblical lines, that authority is more or less centralised than scripture lays down, or that offices and responsibilities are wrongly distributed.

The failure of members to have the ecstatic experiences they feel are their due may be accepted as evidence of there being something amiss in the leader's relationship to God. It may be suggested that the 'Holy Ghost is not with him' or that he is 'not right with God'. I have not heard this advanced as a justification for a breakaway faction while the process of fission was taking place, but it is often advanced by the leader of an established congregation as one reason for his having broken away—after he has done so.

In small sects this is no more than a biblical way of saying 'I want

---

[4] I suspect that this text accounts for the charges of peculation often levelled against leaders by rebellious followers. Even when a Christian is acting in an unChristian fashion he is expected to adhere to a biblical stereotype. Because the Bible says that corrupters of the Gospel are financially dishonest, the saint automatically links heresy with financial dishonesty. It is likely that much the same is true of charges of fornication.

to be independent'. All the sects under discussion claim to be run along strictly biblical lines and the Bible is consulted sometimes when an administrative decision has to be taken. But all the larger ones, with headquarters in the United States, have, over the years, evolved very complex systems of administration which have departed farther and farther from the New Testament model of simplicity.[5] This is of little importance to their branches in England as it is unlikely that more than a handful of their members here have any idea of the complexity of the organisation of their church overseas. They think and act as if the church consisted of its English congregations alone, with a glance now and then at those in the West Indies. For this reason issues of church government over which sects and congregations split are usually ones local to England. Indeed nearly all of them are at congregation level rather than at sect level.

An East London congregation of the Church of God in Christ left the parent body over the issue of church government in 1957, the congregation leader claiming that the sect organisation was more centralised than required by scripture. For two years this congregation operated as an independent sect under the name of the 'All Nations Church of God'; then it joined the New Testament Church of God which is at least as centralised as the sect from which it had originally split. Perhaps the difference was that the leader of the New Testament Church of God in Wolverhampton was farther away than the leader of the Church of God in Christ who lives in London, and therefore less able to interfere in the running of the congregation.

The leader of another breakaway faction gave as his justification the failure of the leader of the parent congregation to 'preach against pride'. This amounted to no more than an accusation, phrased in biblical terms, that he was domineering. I have heard the sin of pride preached against at no sect service I have attended,[6] nor have I heard the leader of the breakaway preach against it at his own services.

Members may withdraw from a congregation simply because it is unsuccessful. To a degree it is felt that a 'work' that has God's blessing cannot be manifestly unsuccessful, and that if it is there must be something amiss in the leader's relationship to God. But this is not necessarily so; lack of success can also be explained by the activities of the Devil or 'a spirit of discord' (i.e., a demon). This can be a

---

[5] The New Testament Church of God has a particularly complex organisation.
[6] Though the virtue of meekness was sometimes extolled in sermons dealing with the Sermon on the Mount.

tribute to the holiness of the leader and his saints, as the Devil is believed to be specially anxious to oppose the work of the very holy leader which he sees as a threat to his own power. It is the duty of the faithful servant of God to put on 'the armour of righteousness' and fight back. This dogma helps congregations to weather the many storms that beset them and provides them with an answer when their competitors accuse them of having lost contact with God.

4. *Doctrinal Disagreement*

Although saints read and reread their Bibles, pray for enlightenment, and discuss difficult passages among themselves, they do not appear to work out new heresies of their own; these are always inspired by reading more or less indiscriminately from the welter of religious magazines and tracts that circulate among them.[7] English Elim publications and to a lesser extent Assemblies of God publications circulate, as do those of many small independent churches and missionary societies operating in almost every country of the world. Important among these are the publications of the Harvest Home Press in London, those of the Slavic Gospel Association, and the *Mount Zion Reporter* which is published by a group of American Pentecostals living in Jerusalem. In addition, saints are likely to read the *Caribbean Challenge*, a mainly religious monthly published in Jamaica which is not exclusively Pentecostal, and therefore a fruitful source of heresy. Apart from 'Newsletters' only one sect brings out a regular publication in England; the quarterly *Church of God Preacher*, edited by the leader of the Church of God of Prophecy.

As well as Pentecostal publications, I have seen those of the Seventh Day Adventists, the Mormons and the Jehovah's Witnesses in the homes of sect members.

The saint who becomes persuaded of the truth of a heresy does not

---

[7] In America the New Testament Church of God, for example, issues the following periodicals:

> *Church of God Evangel* (weekly)
> *The Lighted Pathway* (monthly)
> *Macedonian Call* (quarterly)
> *The Pilot* (quarterly)
> *Church of God Gospel Herald* (monthly, especially for Negroes)

as well as special pamphlets for Sunday Schools. In addition, each State has its own special publication. These find their way into the homes of members and are passed on to others who are not members. This is only one of the American sects publishing periodicals; the total number of them from American Pentecostal churches circulating in England must be nearly a hundred.

promptly withdraw from the sect congregation, nor is he necessarily disfellowshipped. Most heresies add to existing beliefs without conflicting with them, and the sect can afford to permit a degree of heterodoxy among members. They cause dissension only when they have to do with ritual practices, such as baptism, foot-washing or ecstatic experience, as these are felt to be crucial in maintaining a correct relationhip between the saints and God.

The history of the City Mission over the last two years provides two examples of doctrinal disagreement, only one of which led to a permanent split. In both cases there was cause for dissatisfaction with the leadership as well as a suspicion that the congregation was wrong in the doctrine it taught.

The first case involved the young Jamaican who later established the Church of the Living God. He had been converted in Jamaica during his mid-teens at a City Mission service and had become a member. When he came to England in 1955 at the age of seventeen he stayed with a family who were already established here and who had also been City Mission members in Jamaica. Early in 1961 he took to attending services of the Victorious Church of God in Reading and a few months later had established his own congregation there.

At first he almost certainly thought of his new congregation as being a branch of the City Mission and his Reading members used to attend large City Mission meetings in London. Despite his success in establishing a new congregation, he was without rank in the City Mission organisation, so when three City Mission bishops arrived from the West Indies in mid-1961 he asked them to recognise his services by ordaining him. This would have given him a rank higher than that held by anyone else permanently resident in England and they refused to do so. It is possible that they resented his undertaking the establishment of a church without their permission. Being a resourceful young man he journeyed to Wales and persuaded a Welsh Pentecostal pastor to ordain him. His church was already practising the rite of foot-washing, which is at variance with City Mission usage, and at this stage he started expressing doubt about whether it was scriptural to have female bishops. There was already ample doctrinal disagreement to justify the formation of an independent sect.

The final break came after the bishops had returned to the West Indies. As an ordained minister, the Jamaican had made arrangements to conduct the wedding ceremony of a City Mission girl, but the bishops had left instructions that under no circumstances was he to be permitted to do so. So the ceremony was conducted by a Church of England clergyman. After this rebuff he attended only one City Mission service at which he denounced those he considered had been slandering him. At about this time his beliefs began to diverge even further from those of the City Mission; he became convinced that baptism should be in the name of Jesus instead of in the name of Father, Son, and Holy Ghost. In Feburary 1962 he started a Jesus Name congregation in East London and persuaded his Reading congregation to accept the new doctrine.

At the formation of the East London congregation, four nuclear members of the City Mission attended his services. But none of them remained with him long and one of them, the woman whose case is to be discussed next, ultimately returned to the City Mission. By this time his congregation was firmly established and their defection did him little damage.

The next case concerns a middle-aged married woman with a grown family. She had been converted by the City Mission in St. Elizabeth parish, Jamaica, and had brought her husband into the organisation as well. When they migrated to England she started holding services in her home in East London, and it was out of these services that the London congregation of the City Mission grew. Probably because she came from a rural area of Jamaica, remote from the centre of sect activities in Kingston, she held the low rank of 'Worker' in the organisation and when three people arrived from Jamaica who held the superior rank of 'Light Brigade' she recognised their authority and permitted them to take over leadership of the congregation.

Towards the end of 1961 she read a copy of the *Mount Zion Reporter*, mentioned earlier, and became convinced that saints should keep the sabbath in accordance with Old Testament teaching. A few weeks later, the young man who was busy breaking away from the City Mission, and who was her lodger, convinced her of the truth of the Jesus Name doctrine. These two points of disagreement, both of which have a significant bearing on Pentecostal ritual, would normally have led to her withdrawal from the congregation. That, after flirting with the newly formed Jesus Name sect, she is still a member of the City Mission is due partly to her failure to convert her husband, a City Mission deacon, to her point of view, and partly to her strong sense of personal loyalty to the City Mission bishops in Jamaica. In none of my discussions with her during this crisis did she suggest that she intended to break away from the City Mission; she hoped, rather, to win them over to her point of view.[8]

This train of events could hardly have occurred in any of the other sects under discussion. The City Mission is the only sect in England having a system of rank which makes it possible for leaders in Jamaica to appoint leaders in England. In no other congregation would it have been possible for a recent immigrant to take over control from an established congregation leader, as happened in the City Mission, without splitting the congregation.

5. *Processes of Fission*

Sometimes mutual forgiveness and the congregation's confidence that God works in members to dispel ungodly pride and contentiousness do succeed in holding a congregation together; through believing that contention has ceased, the members cease to quarrel. Only a very small proportion of disputes leads to congregation fission or the withdrawal and disfellowshipment of members. The belief, discussed in Chapter VI, (p. 62), that the Church as a group has a special, mystic relationship to God, transcending the relationship of individual members to him, and that it is sinful to disrupt it on trivial grounds, discourages sudden fission in which no attempt is made to heal the breach.

Most splits take place very gradually, months elapsing between the initial disagreement and the first meeting of a separate congregation. We have seen that it took more than a year for the Church of the Living God to separate itself from the City Mission. The sudden and dramatic disfellowshipments in this church, described in this chapter, are the exception rather than the rule. Sometimes a new congregation meets for weeks or even months before its relationship to the parent one is clearly defined. Where, as sometimes happens, the breakaway group draws its members from one locality within the general area in which the parent congregation operates, it can be thought of, for a time, as a daughter congregation rather than as a separate sect. It is likely, though without having observed the process I cannot be certain, that some congregations of multi-congregational sects started as breakaway movements from other, established congregations, were satisfied with partial autonomy, and remained within the sect organisation. Nevertheless, in all cases I recorded as happening during the period of this study, the initial period of uncertainty was

---

[8] But two years later she had converted her husband, broken with the City Mission, and was running her own tiny sect congregation. This still survives (July 1964).

followed by complete autonomy, and the group took a new name.

When fission occurs in this gradual fashion and the congregation becomes established before the formal split occurs, leaders escape the charge of 'walking disorderly' and 'causing dissension in the Church of God'. In its early stages the new congregation can be represented as a missionary endeavour, an attempt to evangelise in a new district, and as such is a meritorious, godly activity. Its true nature is revealed by the presence of few, if any, new members.

The fictional role of daughter congregation given to an emergent independent group is only convincing when members of it come from one district. If they are as geographically dispersed as the members of the parent congregation it is much less plausible, though I have recorded one instance. Here the emergent congregation held meetings a long way from the district in which its members lived and looked at first as if it were evangelising on behalf of the parent congregation.

From this it will be apparent that no clear-cut distinction can be drawn between congregation fission and sect fission; before the split occurs the dissident faction may function separately from the parent one. Because of this, in their initial stages sect fission and sect building are identical processes. In some cases at least the leader of the daughter congregation is not clear whether he wants to lead a congregation within a larger sect organisation or to establish an independent one. How he decides will depend very much on his relationship with the leader of the parent congregation and the willingness of each to compromise. It will also depend on whether disagreement is over church government only, or whether more fundamental issues of the kind discussed earlier in this chapter are involved as well.

6. *Fission and Solidarity*

Although at first sight fission among West Indian Pentecostal sects appears to be entirely disruptive, and is always seen as disruptive by members of a congregation in the process of splitting, it has from a broader viewpoint important integrative functions as well. Indeed conflict between sects and the world, between different sect congregations and within congregations is an essential part of the system. Without the constant turmoil of sect formation, building and fission, members would lose interest and the groups wither and die. Religious enthusiasm is always at its lowest ebb when sect life is jogging along smoothly, and at its peak when there is uncertainty, dissension and fission.

Disputes cause individual members, whether or not they are directly involved, to think about their religious values. If a split occurs they must decide which faction they are to follow and be able to justify their decision to themselves and to other Pentecostals. As we have seen, the issues justifying fission are never fundamental ones. Factions breaking away from a particular sect always remain within the West Indian Pentecostal fold and continue to interact with other sections of it. They consider themselves justified in disrupting God's church precisely because of their passionate adherence to basic Pentecostal beliefs. Disputes and fission stimulate members of both factions to reaffirm their loyalty to group values.

As we have seen, the Bible provides sanctions for both loyalty to the congregation and breaking away from it. Whichever course a member chooses he is reaffirming Pentecostal values and carrying out the will of God. The less willing he is to compromise, the more he is persuaded of his wholehearted dedication to God's service; generally the more contentious he is the more thoroughgoing his allegiance to Pentecostalism. Conflict is part and parcel of religious dedication and enthusiasm.

In addition to the process whereby sects settle down and become increasingly like established denominations, there is a cyclical process of congregation building, explosion and renewal. For months a congregation carries out its regular rituals—members attend two or three times a week, sing, testify and go home again; ecstatic manifestations become less frequent and less convincing. If the congregation does not die quietly (as in Chapter III I have suggested sometimes happens during a hard winter) then sooner or later some member starts to feel dissatisfied and to suspect that there is a fault in the congregation's relationship with God. Tension mounts; and suddenly enthusiasm flares like a bonfire, with disputes, ecstasy and frantic proselytisation. Presently it settles down again with a slightly different personnel; a few members have been recruited, a few peripheral members have become more firmly attached and a few members have broken away.

Although the time the cycle takes varies from congregation to congregation and within the same congregation from year to year, there is a marked tendency for several congregations in the same area to flare up at the same time; one starts and the others follow suit. There is nothing mysterious in this. It is simply that when a congregation flares up it holds larger meetings which require the co-operation of other congregations, who are directly infected with religious enthusiasm. Church of God and Jesus Name congregations, because they practically never hold common meetings, do not appear to influence one another in this way; turmoil involving nearly all the Jesus Name sects in and around London in late 1963 had little effect on the Church of God ones in this area.

In recent years there has been much interest among anthropologists in the integrative function of conflict.[9] This approach seems well suited to the analysis of religious sects, providing one answer to the problem of how they maintain themselves as social systems. But I think caution is needed in applying it to religious groups in general. For example I doubt whether an Anglican congregation would be amenable to this kind of analysis, partly because it does not see itself as being in opposition to society as a whole, partly because it is little preoccupied with strict orthodoxy, but also because members derive satisfaction from belonging to a great number of other, non-religious groups as well; the congregation claims only a small part of their allegiance. Members are less preoccupied with religion than Pentecostals are and they see themselves in non-religious as well as religious roles; often the non-religious roles are more important.

It is likely that Pentecostal sects in later stages of their development fall somewhere between these two poles, that as they become more *denomination*-like and less sect-like conflict diminishes in importance as a mechanism generating social solidarity. I do not think that in the analysis of native English Pentecostal churches (Elim, for example) conflict would prove nearly so important as it is among the West Indians sects I am discussing.

It follows that as West Indian sects settle down in England, establish themselves, and come to own property, so the mechanisms whereby solidarity is maintained will change and conflict diminish in importance. But while the evidence suggests that this is generally true of sect development, some sects, usually but not always large ones, appear to change more rapidly than others. The New Testament Church of God is developing rapidly and has not split in the last two years.

[9] See for example: Fredrik Barth: *Political Leadership Among the Swat Pathans*, L.S.E. Monographs on Social Anthropology, No. 19, 1959: Max Gluckman: *Custom and Conflict in Africa*, Oxford, Basil Blackwell, 1959, and *The Judicial Process among the Barotse of Northern Rhodesia*, Manchester University Press, 1955; Chandra Jayawardena: *Conflict and Solidarity in a Guianese Plantation*, L.S.E. Monographs on Social Anthropology, No. 25, 1963.

VI

DOCTRINE AND IDEOLOGICAL SANCTIONS

As was made clear in my Preface, members of West Indian Pentecostal sects subscribe to the basic tenets of Christianity, which need not be discussed here. Doctrinally the sects are, not surprisingly, closest to the Baptist Church from which they evolved, but certain doctrines and rituals (the two are often inseparable and always closely linked) are peculiar to Pentecostal sects.

Few saints feel themselves part of the general European Christian tradition. To them Christianity, meaning Pentecostal Christianity, started at the beginning of this century, and everything between then and the days of the Apostles was heretical darkness, a turning away from God. For this reason they show no interest in Church history and are outside and unaware of the traditional disputes that divide Christendom. They are vaguely aware that their point of view is more distant from the Roman Catholic one than from that of most Protestant denominations, but none of them knows or really cares what other churches believe.[1] This leads West Indian Pentecostal leaders on pilgrimages to the Holy Land to accept without question relics and monuments which would be rejected as spurious by leaders of most other Protestant denominations.[2]

Unlike most nonconformist groups, West Indian sects are not iconoclastic. They are unaware that iconoclasm ever was an issue, and they have no aversion to religious pictures in their homes and places of worship. Some of these were undoubtedly made for Roman Catholics.

The members of all sects under discussion are biblical fundamentalists. They hold that the Bible is the inspired Word of God and that all of it is literally true. They do, however, distinguish, albeit inconsistently, between the Old Testament as a special dispensation for the Jews before the coming of Christ, and the New Testament which since the coming of Christ has to some extent superseded it. This does not mean that they neglect the Old Testament in favour of the New:

---

[1] At one service the preacher identified the Pope as Anti-Christ.

[2] The City Mission bishops testified to having seen the Virgin Mary's cottage, the tomb of Christ, and other wonders. More original was their interpretation of a recent archaeological excavation at ancient Jericho as the hole into which the walls sank at the sound of Joshua's trumpets.

of the texts read at services over the last two years more than a third came from the Old Testament. Special favourites are Exodus, Daniel and the Psalms.

Members are almost arrogantly uninterested in any knowledge other than biblical and consider the Bible the only fit subject of study for Christians. No members are well educated in the conventional sense and though some leaders have attended Bible Colleges in the United States,[3] these teach little more than familiarity with the Bible. Their leaders have scarcely more theological sophistication than their followers.

'The Bible' means the King James Authorised Version. Members are aware that there are other versions, but these are not used in services. Probably few saints are aware that the Bible as they know it is a translation; some are certainly under the impression that it was originally written in English. Leaders do not see translation as a problem since there is a Pentecostal doctrine that the Word of God is divinely protected against mistranslation; God himself watches over the work of the translator and prevents him from making mistakes.[4]

The saint seeking to understand a passage of scripture approaches the problem ritually, not intellectually. Instead of seeking an answer in a biblical commentary he prays for enlightenment. Indeed he is wary of the more conventional kind of biblical scholarship, suspecting that the Word of God is being replaced by the 'opinions of men': 'Beware lest any man spoil you through philosophy and vain deceit, after the tradition of men, after the rudiments of the world, and not after Christ.' (Colossians ii, 8.) He believes that Scripture can be understood by man only when assisted by the grace of God, and therefore every scriptural interpretation is to some extent a direct revelation from God. The saint holds a doctrine not because he has come to understand it himself by his own efforts, but because God has told him what to believe.

---

[3] Although English Pentecostal churches run Bible Colleges West Indian sect members do not attend them. They prefer to go to the United States for training. One leader has sent two of his children there since he settled in England, but they have remained there.

[4] Bishop Johnson (op. cit.) says: 'Jesus was responsible for that and He quoted this scripture. He said "Heaven and earth shall pass away: but My Word shall not pass away" (Luke xxi, 33). If it was so that some man could take the Bible and change it, taking out of the Bible what God had in it for our learning and now we do not have the right Bible or scriptures, that would make Jesus a liar . . . the devil's purpose is to offset you from the truth of the Bible by telling you that men have changed it. That is a lie. Men could not change it. God guarded and watched over His Word and kept it from passing away.'

This element of divine revelation in the interpretation of Scripture embitters doctrinal disputes. In admitting he is wrong a disputant implies that the Spirit of God has been withdrawn from him. Being mistaken implies lack of holiness, which in turn means loss of prestige.

Every man and woman has the right to interpret Scripture himself by the power of the Holy Spirit, but he is also told in the Bible to bow to the will of those having authority over him. A church (sect congregation) is not simply a group of individuals assembled to worship God as individuals, each for his own religious advancement; it is a mystic entity, the Bride of Christ. It is unscriptural for an individual to worship alone; he must partake with other Christians in the life of the Church. Private supplication and prayer is good but it cannot replace group supplication and praise in a church service. A Christian is enjoined to turn his back on the world, but he must not turn his back on other Christians; having 'Christian fellowship' is both practical and enjoyable—but over and above this it is a religious duty.

This belief is a very powerful integrative force. To divide or disrupt his church is a sin against Christ. Ideally there is no dissension within the church as all members love one another just as they love Jesus. Much is made of the love of members for one another in services; sometimes the pastor will call on those present to shake one another by the hand and say: 'I love you, I am glad you are here,' and members commonly greet one another at services with a kiss. It is considered in extremely bad taste, almost sacrilegious, to express dissension during a service; the two instances of this I recorded were discussed in hushed whispers for weeks. Saints felt them to be terrible scandals.

The insistence on love as a ritual duty and the rather strict patterning of its expression serves to conceal a great deal of genuine affection among members. Love is not only expressed ritually; members choose one another's company rather than the company of other West Indians, they welcome one another in their homes, look after each other's children, help one another to find accommodation and work and sometimes lend or give one another money. Although there is no pooling of economic resources in the Christian church community, members co-operate quite intensively and express their love for one another in non-ritual as well as ritual contexts.

Common devotion to the Bible and Christian love provide the sect congregation with an integrative ideology buttressing the centripetal forces holding it together. Belief in a common doctrine also serves to bind together congregations of the same sect, and to a somewhat lesser extent those of different sects. It is felt proper that Christian congregations should 'have fellowship with one another', providing always that they subscribe to the same or very similar doctrines. How big a doctrinal difference there can be between sects having 'Christian fellowship' depends on circumstances, particularly the private relationship between the leaders, but differences are felt to be slight if they are not expressed in ritual, or are expressed in intermittent rather than regular ritual. Thus congregations of both the New Testament Church of God and the Church of God in Christ, both of which 'wash the feet of saints', have fellowship with the City Mission, which does not. Foot-washing however takes place only at irregular intervals and is not an integral part of every service, so at common services the difference is unobtrusive.

Perhaps the most important sanction these sects derive from the Bible is withdrawal from the world. This is the negative aspect of the positive injunction to organise into churches. The Pentecostal West Indian, and I gather this is true of other Pentecostals as well, thinks very ill of the world, partly (as I shall suggest later) because it does not give him a very large share of the good things it has to offer, but also simply because the Bible tells him to think ill of it. The world is characterised by sin whereas the Church is characterised by avoidance of sin; in keeping with this doctrine every aspect of the world is seen in the worst possible light. A good example of this was the attitude of the Pentecostal saints to the 1962 Cuba crisis; most of them felt that it was sinful for Kennedy and Khrushchev to negotiate to prevent war; this was 'devilish pride', working independently of God. The only proper course for the world leaders was to be 'saved'.[5]

Paul, in his Second Epistle to Timothy, describes the world in the following words: 'For men shall be lovers of their own selves, covetous, boasters, proud, blasphemers, disobedient to parents, unthankful, unholy, without natural affection, trucebreakers, false accusers, incontinent, fierce, despisers of those that are good, traitors, heady, high-minded, lovers of pleasures more than lovers of God; having a

---

[5] In the *Church of God Preacher* (an organ of the Church of God of Prophecy) of June 1961 American space research is discussed: 'The Russians have put a man into space and brought him back again. The Americans, not being outdone have, also, openly, with all who cared to listen, done the same thing although on a smaller scale. That has always been the devil's objective. Anti-Christ will make that his boast "For thou hast said in thine heart, I will ascend into heaven, I will exalt my throne above the stars of God" (Isaiah xiv, 13–15)'. This illustrates well the characteristic Pentecostal attitude to things happening in the world at large.

form of godliness, but denying the power thereof: from such turn away' (II Tim. iii, 2–5). Preachers love quoting this text and insist that because the Bible says the world is like this, it must be so. Theoretically there can be no virtue in it anywhere. Sin can only be avoided by salvation; man is born in sin and must remain, sinning, in the grip of the Devil until delivered by the grace of God manifested in the Blood of the Lamb. Members are certainly uneasy about the admittedly good and kind people they know who are not members of Pentecostal sects. Such people are a challenge to their dogma and perhaps because of them members seize avidly on the tales of murder, theft, ravishing and so forth, reported in the popular Press, as bearing out the Word of God.

Sin to the Pentecostal is estrangement from God. Anything not done by the grace of God is sinful, however 'good' it may appear to be. The everyday categories of 'good' and 'bad' are social, not religious, and 'sin' has no very close relationship to them. When the Pentecostal speaks of avoidance of sin he is talking about a ritual relationship to God, not about his relationship to his fellow men. God looks with favour on those who observe the taboos he arbitrarily imposes; he rewards them with ecstatic religious experiences in this life and with beatification in the next. It is only as rituals whereby God is approached that the taboos of these sects can be understood. The observance of them binds Pentecostals together and further cuts them off from the world, simply because these are taboos that few other people observe.

The sins of special interest to the Pentecostal, those that must ideally be avoided by all saints, are as follows: smoking, drinking, attending film showings and dances, wearing certain kinds of clothes, straightening the hair, and 'fornication'. Although other sins are recognised it is these that are most often discussed.

Smoking and drinking are considered 'unclean' habits inconsistent with the sanctification of the saint's body in the service of God. *Twenty-Nine Important Bible Truths*[6] says: 'The use of tobacco in any form is forbidden as well as the habitual use of narcotics. These sinful practices defile the body, the temple of the Holy Ghost, and are outward evidence of an impure heart. "Having therefore these promises, dearly beloved, let us cleanse ourselves from all filthiness of the flesh and spirit, perfecting holiness in the fear of God" (II Cor. vii, 1). The Bible expressly forbids the use of intoxicating beverages. Even slight

---

[6] A tract of the Church of God of Prophecy setting out the special doctrines of the Churches of God.

indulgence is sinful and not in keeping with scriptural standards of holiness. "Wine is a mocker, strong drink is raging; and whosoever is deceived thereby is not wise" (Proverbs xx, 1)'. My observations of saints in their homes lead me to conclude that these taboos are observed strictly by all of them. Never once have I seen a saint either smoke or drink, nor have I heard rumours that any of them do so.

Attending films and dances is not in quite the same category as smoking and drinking. They are not positive sins but rather activities that show a lack of attachment to God. Instead of attending public entertainments the saint should be praying at home or attending a religious service. Addiction to entertainments shows an inordinate interest in the things of this world. Theoretically the same applies to television, described by one religious leader as 'the lust of the eye', but West Indians have been familiar with television for too short a time for a taboo on it to take root. Some members of sects in London, even nuclear members, have television sets in their houses.

All sects preach against wearing gold jewellery: 'because they are evidences of a prideful heart', they are unbecoming to a child of God. 'Wherefore do ye spend money for that which is not bread? and your labour for that which satisfieth not?' (Isaiah lv, 2). Some of them also preach against other kinds of personal adornment, the 'wearing of fine raiment'. 'In like manner also, that women adorn themselves in modest apparel, with shamefacedness and sobriety; not with broided hair, or gold, or pearls, or costly array.' (I Timothy ii, 9.) But this does not have any very marked effect on the habits of dress of the members who, like all West Indians in England, delight in being well-dressed. A sect service is the occasion for wearing one's best and most colourful clothes.

The objection to hair-straightening is derived from I Timothy ii, 9, quoted above and from I Peter iii, 3. Both of these texts specifically condemn braiding or plaiting the hair, but as the hair of people of African extraction seldom permits of plaiting (though some mothers valiantly try to plait the kinky locks of their daughters) the embargo has been transferred to artificial straightening of the hair which is practised, openly or surreptitiously, by most West Indian women in England.[7] The condemnation of hair-straightening certainly originated with Negro churches in the United States and is not mentioned in the official statements of beliefs of either the New Testament Church of God or the Church of God of Prophecy, most of whose

[7] F. M. Henriques, in *Family and Colour in Jamaica*, London, Eyre and Spottiswoode, 1953, p. 49, says about 75 per cent in Jamaica.

members in the United States are of European extraction. I quote from a broadcast by Bishop Johnson, the leader of a Negro Jesus Name sect, the Church of the Lord Jesus Christ of the Apostolic Faith: 'Is there anyone here tonight guilty of this? Have you lifted up yourself against God?—Saying I'm going to straighten my hair . . . Well God is going to get you.'[8]

Among saints in England it is only nuclear members who follow this taboo faithfully. At any sect service there are women present who have quite clearly straightened their hair, and who do not even attempt to conceal it, as they could by wearing a headscarf. The reason for this is the direct conflict between the taboo and the high value placed on European physical characteristics in Jamaica[9] and other West Indian islands. A saint has to be very thorough-going in her rejection of the world and dedication to God before she gives it up. I suspect that it is easier for a West Indian woman to relinquish the delights of smoking, drinking and fornication than to give up trying to look like a European.

Because sexual irregularities are commonplace in Jamaica, 'fornication' is the most heinous of sins for West Indian sects. I have already shown how even a rumour of sexual irregularity can blight the reputation of a religious leader and cause his following to melt away. This preoccupation undoubtedly arose because of the unusual family organisation of Jamaican peasants. Few couples marry before their children are fully grown, as it is not until then that they can afford the elaborate entertainment considered necessary. As a result nearly all women bear children out of wedlock. As about 70 per cent of children are born out of wedlock the evidences of fornication are obvious.[10] Men are reluctant to undertake the responsibility of marriage and as they have little trouble in finding sexual gratification outside marriage they do not marry. Women are forced to depend on their maternal kin for support unless they can find themselves a permanent man, which they can only do at the risk of bearing still more illegitimate children. This has become a firmly established pattern.

Although their members are drawn from precisely the social class in which this pattern is most common, Pentecostal sects are even less willing to compromise on this issue than are other churches. This is because of their emphasis on the sanctification of the body as the

[8] From the pamphlet entitled *Who is it that Defies and Challenges the Whole Religious World on these Subjects?*, described as '1958 revised edition' and apparently printed for this sect in Philadelphia.

[9] Henriques, *Family and Colour in Jamaica*, pp. 47 ff.

[10] See Henriques, op. cit., Chapter 5, for a detailed account.

temple of God. 'Flee fornication. Every sin that a man doeth is without the body; but he that committeth fornication sinneth against his
own body. What? know ye not that your body is the temple of the
Holy Ghost which is in you, which ye have of God, and ye are not
your own?' (I Cor. vi, 18–19). Clearly freedom from the ritual im-
purity associated with fornication is absolutely essential if the object
of sect ritual is to be achieved. The Holy Ghost will not inhabit a
temple that has been defiled and the member will not be blessed with
ecstatic experience. As it is felt that one impure member in a congregation is sufficient to preclude the presence of the Holy Ghost at
services, it is in the interests of each member to see that others do not
fornicate. For this reason I think the actual behaviour of sect members is very close to the ideal.

'Fornication' for these sects includes pre-marital intercourse,
extra-marital intercourse and the remarriage of people who are
divorced. Divorce and remarriage are allowed only if husband or wife
has committed 'fornication' and even then are unlikely. 'But I say
unto you, that whosoever shall put away his wife, saving for the cause
of fornication, causeth her to commit adultery: and whosoever shall
marry her that is divorced committeth adultery.' (Matt. v, 32.) The
word 'fornication' here is interpreted by the Church of God of
Prophecy as bigamy; therefore to divorce a wife who is merely un-
faithful is forbidden. Before this can be done she must be married to
someone else, which is so unlikely that divorce is practically impossible.

Having committed fornication in the past does not disqualify one
from becoming a sect member, any more than having been a smoker
or drinker does. Certainly many women members in England have
pre-marital children in the West Indies. But once one is a member
fornication must be abjured for good. One slip may, perhaps, be
forgiven, but it is not possible for a saint to sin again and again and as
often as he sins be reconverted and readmitted into the fellowship of
the saints. It is a much more serious affront to God for a saint to sin
than for an unsaved person to do so: 'For it is impossible for those
who were once enlightened, and have tasted of the heavenly gift, and
were made partakers of the Holy Ghost, and have tasted the good word
of God, and the powers of the world to come, if they shall fall away,
to renew them again unto repentance; seeing they crucify to themselves the Son of God afresh, and put him to an open shame' (Heb.
vi, 4–6).

In practice this harsh doctrine is tempered with mercy. It can be
interpreted as applying not to those who have simply been 'saved' but

only to those who have been baptised in the Spirit. As I have shown elsewhere there is often doubt about whether a particular saint has been baptised in the Spirit.[11] If he backslides and seeks readmittance to the church he can be given the benefit of the doubt. I have recorded numerous instances of backsliding saints being reconverted.

Despite their insistence on strict adherence to Scripture and a predilection for St. Paul that will be obvious from the numerous quotations from his Epistles in this chapter, none of the sects under consideration considers celibacy in itself as a Christian virtue. Despite Paul's glorification of celibacy and acceptance of marriage as only a second-best, as a practical means of avoiding fornication (I Cor. vii), to the saints marriage is a normal and holy state and sex within marriage is not sinful. Very nearly all leaders of sect congregations in England are married, many of them with large families, and the married mother, especially if she is getting on in years, is much respected.

However, although marriage is pleasing to God, marriage with non-believers is not, and ideally Pentecostal sects are endogamous. Paul counsels endogamy in quite unequivocal terms: 'Be ye not unequally yoked together with unbelievers: for what fellowship hath rightousness with unrighteousness? and what communion hath light with darkness?' (II Cor. vi, 14.) Most marriages are endogamous within the general West Indian Pentecostal group, but not always within the same sect or congregation. As I have already suggested, when a Christian married a non-Christian there was a marked tendency for the non-Christian spouse to be brought within the sect's orbit.

A saint married to an unbeliever may not desert his wife but should rather use the intimacy of the marriage relationship to bring about her conversion. (I Cor. vii, 12–17.) Of course, this applies to marriage only, and not to other kinds of sexual liaison, which should be either sanctified forthwith or dissolved.

All the sects under discussion are millennial; this belief adds a sense of urgency to injunctions of withdrawal from the world and sin. As Christ is likely to come suddenly and without warning, every saint must live in a state of preparedness, must strive constantly to preserve the ritual relationship to God which will ensure his prompt salvation.

The extreme sinfulness of the world and the falling away of people from God in traditionally Christian countries are accepted as indications that the Second Coming cannot be very distant: 'Now the Spirit speaketh expressly, that in the latter times some shall depart

[11] See Chapter VII.

from the faith, giving heed to seducing spirits, and doctrines of devils'[12] (I Tim. iv, 1), and 'Let no man deceive you by any means; for that day shall not come, except there come a falling away first, and that man of sin be revealed, the son of perdition'. (II Thess. ii, 3.)

Saints identify themselves with 'them which were sealed', with those who are not destined to undergo the fiery tribulations described in the Apocalypse. When Christ comes in the air the saints will be snatched up to dwell forever with him in glory. (I Thess. iv, 16–17.) 'These are they which came out of great tribulation, and have washed their robes, and made them white in the blood of the Lamb.' (Rev. vii, 14.)

It is part of traditional Pentecostal doctrine that the resurrected saints, and those who are living when Christ arrives, shall return to earth to rule with him for a thousand years, and that not until these thousand years are expired will the unhallowed dead be resurrected, summarily judged and cast into the lake of fire. But this is unimportant to sect members, whose interest generally extends no farther than the first resurrection in which they are confident of participating. Not once has the second resurrection and the thousand years' reign of Christ been the subject of a sermon or testimony at a service I have attended.

It is difficult to estimate just how important millennial doctrine is in the life of saints, but it appears to be more significant as an ideological sanction for the maintenance of separation from the world than as a principle governing their day-to-day operation. As I have shown, sects strive to establish themselves firmly, making plans for the future and buying property. Individual members also plan for the future, buy property, establish homes and bring their children and other relatives from the West Indies. In this they behave just as non-Pentecostal West Indians do.

This is seen in their approach to recruitment, other aspects of which have been discussed earlier in this chapter. On the one hand they almost welcome the lack of interest of the general population in religion, since it indicates that the millennium is about to arrive, but on the other hand they deplore the situation and try to remedy it by evangelism. This ambivalence accounts for the sporadic nature of proselytisation; for months a congregation will turn in on itself, will 'watch and pray', waiting for Christ to arrive. Then, quite suddenly, it will turn its attention outwards; saints will start praying for revival and calling for it in their testimonies and sermons. Presently they will

[12] The second sermon quoted in Appendix VIII illustrates this belief.

become convinced that it is the will of God and will hold 'campaigns' and meetings on street corners in an endeavour to make new converts.

Certainly the absence of a clear directive from God is often a rationalisation of the group's failure to proselytise in any thorough-going fashion, and I suspect some members realise this. The saint's attitude to proselytisation is ambivalent: on the one hand it is an activity directed towards increasing the congregation's membership, but on the other it is a ritual in itself pleasing to God, and it really does not matter whether converts are made or not, as long as saints stand up and testify.

This draws attention to a basic conflict in the ideology of all the groups under discussion. They think of themselves as an exclusive band destined to be plucked out of the world on the Day of Judgement, a select few who can never be more than a few because the Book of Revelation speaks specifically (Rev. vii, 4) of the 'hundred and forty and four thousand' of 'them which were sealed'.[13] But at the same time they must follow Christ's injunction to preach the Word, to make converts, to bring as many as possible to the 'Mercy Seat'.[14] In structural terms, they are minority groups all of whose activities are geared to fulfilling the needs of a minority, but they are also part-inheritors of the long-universal religious tradition of Europe. In their testimonies at services members speak both of the imminent Second Coming and of the Great Revival which will, if the saints pray hard enough, transform the world into a Pentecostal paradise.

Revival must always await the will of God. It is sacrilegious for man to act without him and before starting a campaign saints must have a 'sign'. Uncertainty as to the will of God is often advanced as justification for the congregation's turning in on itself and for the very haphazard way in which congregations undertake evangelism. Few campaigns are adequately planned and those who show interest in becoming sect members are seldom consistently followed up. Reliance is placed on the working of the 'Holy Spirit' to consolidate the allegiance of those who have been 'saved' at campaign meetings, and when they fail to attend regular services this is accepted as being the 'will of God'. I have often received the impression that members are

---

[13] It has never been suggested to me that Pentecostals should cease preaching the Word when their church has 144,000 members.

[14] This arises from the ritual aspects of evangelism. The preaching of the Word is, in itself, a ritual pleasing to God, so members are not necessarily disappointed when they fail to make converts. They accept that it is not the will of God that they should do so. This passive acceptance of failure effectively prevents consistent, energetic proselytisation.

not really trying, that revival is a group ritual undertaken for its own sake and that like the regular service it is more concerned with the solidarity of the group than with extending its boundaries.

This view was borne out by the very spectacular campaign run by the City Mission in East London in 1961 which drew crowds of up to six hundred. Members did attempt to note the names and addresses of the strangers who attended but this was done very half-heartedly. Members were far too involved in the rituals of praying, testifying and receiving blessings to pay much attention to strangers while the meetings were in progress. After the campaign attendance fell off sharply, and within a few months it was at the same level as before the campaign started. In terms of recruitment it was an utter failure, but members recall with nostalgia the large crowds, the atmosphere of almost hysterical excitement, and the outpouring of the Holy Spirit. Ritually they consider it to have been a success. It was pleasing to God.

Hellfire is not very often talked about in sect services. Although members believe in a literal hell, a place of punishment where the unsaved go after death, they are not over-interested in it. The emphasis is more on the alienation of the unsaved from God than on their eternal punishment. Members very often talk about the delights of heaven which they expect to enjoy when they die or when Christ comes, but the fate of other people is taken for granted and little discussed.

Lack of interest in the theme of eternal punishment may perhaps be explained by the sects' view that the reward of the Christian begins in this life. It is not only after he is dead that a saint begins to reap the reward of his devotion; God watches over him while he is still alive and confers blessings such as ecstasy and healing on him. The life of the Church is, in a sense, a prototype of the state of blessedness in which saints will dwell in heaven. Testimonies, sermons and private conversations all confirm the view that members conceive of heaven as a celestial Pentecostal meeting, in which the saints will 'spend eternity singing around the Throne'.

VII

RITUAL

1. *Introduction*

A SECT congregation meets to perform rituals which, as I have shown in Chapter VI, are sanctioned by its interpretation of passages of Scripture, and only passages which permit of translation into ritual are felt to be important. Members do not distinguish between belief and ritual; to them belief itself, and the reading of the Bible that gives rise to beliefs, are in themselves ritual acts. A Christian or 'saint' is not one who subscribes to West Indian Pentecostal beliefs, but one who takes part in the ritual, and the emphasis is always on doing rather than on believing. I have seldom been asked in the course of this study 'Do you believe in such and such a doctrine?' but very often 'Do you perform such and such a ritual?' 'Do you wash the feet of the saints?' for example. No West Indian Pentecostal leader is prepared to admit that one who is 'saved', who 'has accepted Jesus' is bound for heaven unless he does something about it; unless he is baptised according to a strictly prescribed ritual:

> There has been not one baptism performed RIGHT for more than fifteen hundred years, unless it was done according to Acts ii, 38. . . . Jesus said, 'Except a man be born of the water and spirit he cannot enter into the Kingdom of God' (John iii, 5). Therefore, this leaves the religious world out of the plan of salvation according to the words of Jesus. The modern way of today in converting men and women to Christ is unscriptural, such as: joining a Church; raising the hand and accepting Christ as your personal Saviour. . . . Every man and woman that has not been baptised according to Acts ii, 38 and received the Holy Ghost according to Acts ii, 4, is still in their sins.[1]

Members do not think of their sects as simply one branch of Christianity among many others; they are the only true branch. Members of other churches (with the possible exception of some Pentecostal ones) are, with pagans, Communists and atheists, bound for hell. Only those who perform the appropriate Pentecostal rituals can

---

[1] From the pamphlet *Who is it that Defies and Challenges the Whole Religious World on these Subjects?*, by Bishop Johnson, Philadelphia, 1958 (no publisher).

escape hell, and there is no possibility of compromise with God; the Bible tells the believer what ritual acts he must perform and failure to do so is disobedience to God.

Everything that takes place in the service is a ritual act, very strictly patterned: certainly innovations creep unnoticed into the conduct of services because they are convenient, but strictly speaking, only acts sanctioned by Holy Writ should be permitted. Saints are constantly contrasting man-made 'customs' of other churches with their own strict adherence to Biblical injunctions. At the same time, they contrast the spontaneity of their services with the formality of the services of other churches. They insist on the freedom of their members to worship 'as the Spirit leads'.

It is true that members are expected to participate to a greater extent than they can in most other churches, but the manner of their participation is hedged round by custom: a leader 'preaches' or 'exhorts' from a rostrum whereas a member 'testifies' from the body of the hall. Testimonies are separated by hymns. A member cannot testify as soon as another has finished doing so, but must wait for the hymn to be sung. The sentiments expressed in them and the vocabulary used are all but identical. Members, who use West Indian dialect among themselves before and after services, avoid using it as much as they can when testifying or preaching, and by so doing recognise the formality of the occasion. Dance steps employed in 'dancing in the Spirit' are always the same or very similar, as are the phonetics of of the 'unknown tongues' spoken by members in ecstasy.[2]

These are examples chosen at random. Practically every act during services is governed by convention and members seldom fail to behave in terms of it. Sects disagree and split over complexes of ritual behaviour, but where a complex is accepted the details of its performance are generally identical from sect to sect.[3] Thus, sects that wash the feet of saints (all of them but the City Mission) perform the rite in exactly the same way whether they are Church of God or Jesus Name churches; churches that formally take up offerings follow the same ritual in collecting and consecrating them. Even groups of churches that think of themselves as fundamentally different, as do the Jesus Name and Church of God branches, share a common body of ritual practices, so much so that it is often impossible to say which group a particular congregation belongs to, simply from attending its

[2] Examples are provided in Appendix V.
[3] Except that some Jesus Name churches have their own way of celebrating Holy Communion.

services. In ritual any one West Indian Pentecostal church is much more like any other than it is like non-West Indian ones.

The rituals are directly and consciously concerned with the solidarity of the group of worshippers, especially the nuclear members. Solidarity does not come about incidentally, but is consciously engineered and is itself a group value. The kind of service felt to be truly successful is one in which the congregation responds unanimously and spontaneously to the exhortations and ritual statements and acts of the leader, in which members spring to their feet as one man and shout 'Praise the Lord' till the building shakes, in which the congregation rocks and stamps in time to the cadence of the preacher's voice.

The congregation's uninhibited unanimous participation is a prerequisite to the 'falling of the Spirit'; in fact it is really the same thing. A meeting in which members feel the presence of their God is one in which they feel solidarity with their fellows, and all the preacher's efforts are directed towards this aim. A successful leader is one who can stimulate his congregation to respond as a group, who can make members lose their own individuality in an impassioned, sometimes hysterical identification with the church. Of course, not all services achieve this ideal, but it is achieved sufficiently often for most members to have experienced it and to strive to experience it again.

The high point of a successful service is the member's experience of the presence of God and identification with the church; and all group rituals, prayers, testimonies and exhortations are directed towards achieving this. The orientation of ritual towards this one object is remarkably coherent and consistent; this, for the sect member, is what his religion is about. It has little to do with ethics, theology or beliefs, it is concerned almost obsessively with this relationship with the group and with God. Ethics, theology or beliefs are important only in so far as they contribute to this. The member is quite uninterested in the philosophical correlates of Christianity; in fact, as I have suggested, he is suspicious of them, he suspects that they may betray him to the Devil, that they may come between him and his experience of God. He is equally unconcerned with his relationship to society; he is willing to offer his own magico-religious panaceas for the ills of the world, but as the world is manifestly unwilling to accept them, he turns his back on it.

Morals and ethics are not, for the West Indian Pentecostal, much concerned with his relationship to his fellow men; they are much more a matter of his relationship to God. He does not forego sin because it is wrong in any social sense, but because it is offensive to his deity. The sins which are often the subject of Pentecostal sermons are those mentioned in the Bible, and little attempt is made to re-interpret these in terms of an industrialised society, nor is there any appreciation of the comparative gravity of sins; a preacher will mention in the same breath the wickedness of murder and the wicked-ness of woman's straightening her hair or coming to church without a hat. Avoidance of sin is a negative ritual, perhaps a purification, that enables the saint to approach God. If he has observed the negative rituals then he can feel more confident that the positive ones will be efficacious in achieving this object. Ultimately for the saint sin is not action or failure to act, but a state of being alienated from God and the group of worshippers. Those who live in the world are sinful not because they commit sins but because they have not taken the ap-propriate ritual steps to rid themselves of sin. Just as the avoidance of sin is a ritual pleasing to God, so those who have sinned can shed their sins by submitting to the appropriate ritual, making themselves acceptable to God and to God's church. Salvation, baptism and baptism of the Spirit, the inductive sin-removing rituals, are neces-sary steps in the individual's approach to God and acceptance into the group of worshippers.

Everyone becoming a member of a congregation must pass through these rituals before he can play a full and effective part in the regular recurrent rituals enabling the congregation to approach their God. Theoretically at least, it is as important to the congregation that re-cruits be fully inducted as it is to the neophyte. The Holy Ghost is more likely to fall on a congregation all of whose members have passed through the sin-shedding rites than on one which includes people who are unsaved or unbaptised. I have heard the presence of unbelievers put forward as a reason for the Holy Ghost failing to fall or failing to heal sick members, but I have not heard incredulity expressed when the Holy Ghost did fall in meetings attended by unbelievers. Little is made of this doctrine, probably because an insistence on it would make proselytisation difficult. This is a further aspect of the am-bivalent attitude to proselytisation already discussed. To be thorough-ly in contact with God, saints must avoid contact with the world; but only by contact with the world, in the person of the unsaved, can the congregation recruit.

2. *Regular Rituals*

Congregation rituals can conveniently be divided into those which are performed regularly at every service and those which are per-

formed periodically, at some services only. Regular rituals comprise
nearly everything that happens at a service, as there is little if any
religious behaviour which is not ritualised. Here I am going to discuss
the more important blocks of ritual behaviour—ritual complexes—
and suggest what they mean to the people who perform them, and
their function in group solidarity. They are: testimony, prayer,
preaching and exhortation, talking with tongues and other ecstatic
behaviour, singing, congregation responses, reading from Scripture
and invocation.

Testimony

All members testify at services.[4] If the congregation is a very small
one nearly every member testifies at every service, but in larger congregations there is not enough time for this. Those who testify are
predominantly nuclear members, some of whom will testify at service
after service, week after week. An ordinary member does so less
frequently, but this is partly because he attends fewer services. Table 9

TABLE 9

*Frequency of Testimony, Nuclear and Ordinary Members
January and February, 1961*

Meeting	A	B	C	D	E	F	G	H	I	J	K	L	M	N	O	P	Q	R	S	T	U	V
Nuclear Members																						
Attendance	7	9	7	18	10	10	16	18	5	8	10	19	15	5	8	7	15	14	5	9	10	10
Testimony	5	6	6	8	5	6	9	6	4	7	7	7	7	4	7	6	8	8	4	8	7	8
Ordinary Members																						
Attendance	1	3	4	6	6	0	4	6	0	0	1	8	4	2	0	2	4	1	0	5	5	1
Testimony	1	1	1	2	3	0	1	2	0	0	0	2	1	2	0	2	1	0	0	0	1	0
Totals																						
Attendance	8	12	11	24	16	10	20	24	5	8	11	27	19	7	8	9	19	15	5	14	15	11
Testimony	6	7	7	10	8	6	10	8	4	7	8	9	8	6	7	8	9	8	4	8	8	8

[4] Examples of testimony will be found in Appendix V.

indicates the frequency with which nuclear and non-nuclear members testified at City Mission meetings in 1961. Testimonies are also acceptable from visiting members of other sects and even from people who consider themselves Christians but who do not belong to a sect congregation, as it is always hoped that these will later become members. Testimonies are nearly always volunteered, though at very big meetings it may be agreed beforehand that certain members will testify to stimulate others present to do the same. The congregation leader seldom calls on members to testify but he presides over the testimonies, seeing that they are given in an orderly fashion, that two people do not testify at once. Where two people stand up to testify it is his duty to indicate which of them shall speak first.

A testimony can either be spoken or sung. This makes it possible for the member who finds difficulty in expressing himself to participate equally with the others. A sung testimony consists of a hymn, usually one chosen from the Sankey or Redemption hymn books. The testifier sings the first verse or so on his own, and then the congregations joins in, supporting him and so reducing his nervousness and embarrassment at being the centre of attention. He then says a few words before returning to his seat.

The spoken testimony ranges between the gabbled recitation of a fixed formula and a long harangue exhorting members to be faithful to God. Generally it is ordinary members who deliver the first type of testimony and nuclear ones the second, but most fall between these two extremes. The testimony is supposed to give thanks to Jesus for the testifier's salvation, and to state in very general, strictly patterned terms 'what God has done for me'.[5] Sometimes testifiers refer to specific instances of divine intervention in their lives, such as healing, or they give a circumstantial account of their own salvation or of their baptism in the Spirit, but this is unusual. Most references to actual events are generalised and stylised.

Testimony provides an opportunity for every member to be the centre of attention during the service and to make an individual, unique contribution to it. Some testimonies tail off into talking in tongues and many testifiers twitch ritually as they testify, so that the testimony further provides an opportunity for members to demonstrate in front of the congregation that they are specially blessed by God. There is considerable pressure on members to testify. Testifying is 'doing something for God', and he who consistently fails to testify

---

[5] Examples are found in the testimony in Appendix V.

is suspected of being lukewarm in his loyalty to both God and the church, as testimony is an affirmation of both these loyalties.

Talking with Tongues (glossolalia)

The majority (perhaps all) of ejaculations in tongues (examples of which will be found in Appendix VI) are quite conscious and intentional; they take place at appropriate moments in testimony or prayer and sometimes provide a 'fill-in' when the saint runs out of words; he talks with tongues while he thinks what he is going to say next. In the service they have precisely the same function as ejaculations of 'Praise the Lord', 'Hallelujah', and so forth: they provoke a similar response from those listening, maintain the speaker's *rapport* with his audience, and encourage participation. Like ejaculations of praise they are conventionally believed to be involuntary, as it is believed that God directly inspires members to praise him. When asked the meaning of an ejaculation, a saint either says that he does not know or that it is 'praise'.

Apart from these short ejaculations, less than a quarter of the members indulge in quite lengthy talking with tongues which can last for up to four minutes but average about a minute. These have a different function from the short ejaculations: they are primarily intended to impress the congregation with the holiness of the talker and the closeness of his contact with God. Usually he has reason to feel his position in the congregation threatened in some way, perhaps because of a quarrel or disagreement with another member, so in this context talking in tongues is a way of restoring his confidence in himself, justifying himself before the other members and, perhaps, ritually 'putting down' the person with whom he has quarrelled.[6]

There remain the very rare instances of what appear to be quite involuntary talking with tongues. These are not easily distinguished from those discussed above; not knowing the social context of an outbreak of talking with tongues, the observer can easily be misled into thinking it unpremeditated and involuntary. This is particularly so since simulated nervous exhaustion is an integral part of the ritual. A member who has talked with tongues seldom resumes normal participation in the service immediately, but sags in his chair or kneels on the floor. He does not take part in the hymn or chorus that usually follows talking in tongues but interrupts it with groans or ejaculations of 'Praise the Lord'.

Perhaps because calculated talking with tongues is so closely

[6] This aspect of talking with tongues is discussed in Chapter VI.

associated with the internal disputes and rivalries of the sect nucleus, the apparently involuntary talker with tongues is seldom a member of it. The three instances of talking with tongues I witnessed which appeared to be involuntary all involved members who were not nuclear. It is not improbable that by talking with tongues one who is not very firmly attached to a congregation asserts his holiness *vis à vis* nuclear members who tend to monopolise the proceedings; at the same time he demonstrates his loyalty to the congregation and perhaps his resolve to participate more intensively in future. If this is so, talking with tongues can be a way of claiming a place in the nucleus. But I recorded so few instances that I cannot be certain of this.

Interpretation of tongues is very rare in these sects. In this they differ from the English Pentecostal Elim Church, which places great emphasis on interpretation in keeping with St. Paul's injunction to the church at Corinth:

'For he that speaketh in an unknown tongue speaketh not unto men, but unto God: for no man understandeth him; howbeit in the spirit he speaketh mysteries.' (I Cor. xiv, 2.) 'I would that ye all spake in tongues, but rather that ye prophesied: for greater is he that prophesieth than he that speaketh with tongues, except he interpret, that the church may receive edifying.' (I Cor. xiv, 5.)

And again: 'Wherefore let him that speaketh in an unknown tongue pray that he may interpret.' (I Cor. xiv, 13.)

Elim Pentecostals insist that every message in tongues must be interpreted and that talking with tongues must not be permitted to dominate the service: 'If any man speak in an unknown tongue let it be by two, or at most by three, and that by course; and let one interpret. But if there be no interpreter, let him keep silence in the church; and let him speak to himself, and to God.'

Such strict regulation of the gift of tongues is probably only possible in a church which, like Elim, has a strong central organisation. West Indian Pentecostal leaders never tire of telling their congregations that all things must be done 'decently and in order' (I Cor. xiv, 40), but they lack the authority to prevent members talking with tongues when they feel so inclined, and they cannot insist on interpretation unless they do it themselves. A leader who 'silences' a talker with tongues may be suspected of jealousy and accused of acting counter to scripture, for Paul says also: 'Covet to prophesy, and forbid not to speak with tongues.' As we have seen, speaking in tongues may be competitive, so it is unlikely that one member will back up another's speaking in tongues by interpreting for him; he is more likely to try to be even with him by speaking in tongues himself.

On only one occasion have I witnessed interpretation of tongues by someone other than the person who had spoken. Leaders, perhaps because they are better acquainted with Scripture, but mainly because they feel personally responsible for the performance of ritual 'decently and in order', sometimes interpret after they have themselves spoken with tongues.

In another section I have drawn attention to the disintegrative functions of ecstatic behaviour, especially talking with tongues.[7] I have suggested that members make use of ecstasy to assert their outstanding holiness *vis-à-vis* other members, but it has integrative functions as well. Where the ecstatic is the leader of the congregation, as is often the case, his ecstasy is intended to, and often does, unite congregation support behind him. Ecstasy is a ritual way of repudiating disintegration, of affirming the group's solidarity, its common beliefs and common goal in communion with its God. In very large meetings, talking with tongues is exclusively an integrative ritual. Here there is no point in a member's seeking support by demonstrating his holiness, as relatively few of those present can be aware of internal congregation politics. Also, as I have suggested, at a large meeting many of those who talk with tongues are not nuclear members of the sect, and perhaps not even ordinary members.

Dancing in the Spirit

'Dancing in the Spirit', involuntary twirling and prancing, is also accepted as a 'blessing', a manifestation of the Holy Ghost. Like talking in tongues it occurs in mild and acute forms. At many services saints stand and dance in the one spot without leaving their places. Sometimes they remain seated and stamp rhythmically. This usually occurs when the atmosphere of the service is highly charged and a 'blessing' is expected. By dancing and stamping members show their satisfaction with the service and that they are 'happy in the Lord'.

The only instance of involuntary dancing I have witnessed was quite different from this. The dancer, a girl in her late 'teens', was anxious about her health and had sought faith-healing for persistent headaches. With eyes tightly closed she twirled frantically in the clear space between the front row of chairs in the hall and the platform on which the leaders were sitting. Men in the congregation pushed her away from chairs and walls against which she could have hurt herself,

[7] See Chapter VI.

1. Leading the singing

2. Sung testimony

but did not attempt to restrain her. An elderly woman calmly collected her shoes when she lost them. Finally she fell exhausted to the
floor and remained lying there motionless for the duration of the
service.

Ritual Twitching

Ritual twitching or shuddering is commonplace at all sect services,
though not all members twitch and shudder. This, like short ejaculations in tongues, is meant to indicate that the person concerned is
being moved by the Holy Ghost, that he is being 'blessed'. Those who
twitch and shudder usually ejaculate in tongues as well.

Prayer

Prayers can be offered by one saint or by all members of the congregation together. When the leader prays on behalf of the congregation or asks a member to do so, or a member offers a prayer dedicating
the offering, the rite is normally performed standing up, often with
arms raised and outstretched. Other members also stand, bow their
heads and repeat the closing 'Amen'.

In group prayer each member kneels in front of the chair in which
he has been sitting and either rests both elbows on it cradling his
head in his hands or slumps over it. Each saint prays on his own
account, some quietly and some very loudly. Generally nuclear
members pray loudest and longest, continuing after others have
finished. It is not until the last of them has said 'Amen' that all those
present raise their heads and the prayer is finished. In addition,
members kneel individually and pray quietly for about a minute
before sitting down at the commencement of a service, especially if
they arrive after it has begun, as many of them do.

Sometimes a prayer, whether individual or communal, is for something specific. Nearly all the specific prayers I have recorded asked
God to heal a member of the congregation, usually one who was too
ill to attend the service or was in hospital. On one occasion the prayer
was for a member's relative in Jamaica. All the rest asked for the
'deliverance' of a member from some emotional problem. In non-
specific prayers the saint is talking to God rather than asking him for
something; so they are comprised of profuse, patterned thanks for
the member's salvation and the many 'blessings' conferred on him
and on the Church.

Testimonies are phrased in everyday speech (though as I have said
not in dialect) profusely interwoven with quotations from Scripture,

but prayers are phrased as far as the member can manage, in the 'biblical' language of the King James Bible. In his testimony the saint is talking to other saints but in prayer he is talking to God, so a special ritual language is employed.[8]

Members can testify only in services, but they are expected to pray outside services as well as in them. One woman described how she spent her lunch hour at work praying, apparently much to the embarrassment of her non-Pentecostal work-mates; a man claimed that he sometimes prayed all night instead of sleeping. The City Mission organised a 'Band of Prayer'; each day every member was to stop what he was doing at an agreed hour and pray, as it was felt that such concerted prayer at the same time stood a better chance of capturing the attention of God than did the individual prayers of members at different times. Leaders continually reminded members during services of the time at which they should pray, and appealed to them not to 'break our chain of prayer'.

Although some prayers are requests for divine intervention in specific circumstances, most can only be classed as rituals of solidarity; the member, in his prayers whether during a service or alone, is reaffirming group values and demonstrating his loyalty to them. This is particularly so in the 'Band of Prayer' described above. Here the member knows that other members are performing the same ritual at the same time; although he may be alone he is participating in a common ritual.

Preaching and Exhortation

The only distinction between 'testifying' and 'preaching' is the formal one that testimonies are given from the body of the hall whereas preaching is carried out from the rostrum. Some testimonies exhort members to be faithful to God and the Church, just as some preaching is mainly concerned with the personal testimony.

Preaching and exhortation are terms used interchangeably by sect members for any address delivered from the stage of a hall or from behind a table if there is no stage. A few make the distinction that one 'preaches' to the unsaved and 'exhorts' the saints, but this is not general.

All congregation leaders preach and in most congregations some nuclear members do so too.[9] Sometimes these are given the special title of 'evangelist'. Sermons (called 'the message') are preached without notes, partly because it is believed that the Holy Ghost inspires

[8] Examples of prayers are given in Appendix VII.
[9] Examples of preaching are in Appendix VIII.

the preacher directly, and tells him what to say. Usually a text is taken (often from a passage read earlier in the service) but the preacher uses it more as an incantation than as a means of communication. I have heard very few sermons that really tried to enlighten members, to deepen their appreciation of the meaning of Scripture. Most sermons, like testimonies, are mainly directed towards arousing a response in the congregation, quickening their awareness of God. The successful sermon is not one that has been well thought out, but rather one that stimulates members to shout 'Praise the Lord' and perhaps have ecstatic experiences.

At regular congregation services only one sermon is preached by the congregation leader, but at longer services attended by the leaders of other congregations, three or four are not unusual. At these longer meetings visiting celebrities are invited to sit on the platform with the congregation leader, and each of them expects to be given a part to play in the service. The number of sermons that must be preached at large meetings is one of the factors that make agreements to end meetings at a particular hour so irksome, and is thus indirectly responsible for the attempts of so many congregations to buy their own premises.

In his sermon the leader expresses for congregation members what they all think and feel. He reiterates ritually the beliefs of the group, which expresses its concurrence and approval by ritual interjections. No sermon is complete without these; they allow the preacher to gauge the degree of *rapport* he has established and preach accordingly—progressively working up the congregation's enthusiasm.

Congregation responses are few and conventionalised. They are: 'Yes!' 'True!' 'Amen!' 'Praise Him!' 'Praise the Lord!' 'Praise His Name!' 'Hallelujah!' and 'Thank you Jesus!' Sometimes the preacher takes the congregation through its paces by asking them to stand and say 'Praise the Lord'—he says it first and the congregation repeats it after him.[10] He is most likely to do this if it is evident that *rapport* is not being maintained and enthusiasm is flagging; some preachers do it almost as a matter of course, before they start preaching—possibly because it is difficult to preach this kind of sermon unless there is active support from the congregation.

Most sermons are rhythmical repetitions of stock phrases and sentiments, normally punctuated by one or two of the response phrases listed above. The preacher's use of one of these gives the congregation its cue and they shout it after him, although sometimes the congrega-

---

[10] This is the noisiest part of any service and the aspect of West Indian Pentecostal worship that is likely to bring protests from neighbours (see Chapter IV, p. 33).

tion responds spontaneously with no cue except a pause in the speaker's delivery. In many services there is a self-appointed response leader and the congregation takes its cue from him, but this is quite informal and nobody present is aware of following a leader. The response leader is either the visiting leader of another congregation or a nuclear member of the host congregation. During one service several different people may fill this role. The success of a sermon depends on the co-operation of the congregation. The preacher presides over the congregation's ritual expression of its solidarity through devotion to God, rather than acting on its behalf. Preaching and response are integral parts of the same rite.

Hymns

Singing occupies about half the time of the service, which starts with a religious song and ends in most sects with a special doxology, 'Praise God From Whom All Blessings Flow', which is sung at no other time. Religious songs are divided into two classes, 'hymns' and 'choruses'; hymns are felt to be the more holy. Whereas choruses are sung sitting down, hymns are sung standing up, but this rule is not invariably observed.

About nine-tenths of the hymns sung during services are taken from the 'Sankey' or 'Redemption' hymn books, which are used by other Pentecostal churches as well; of the other tenth some appear to be peculiar to the West Indies. Although most members know the words of the hymns by heart, they always use hymn books, and the leader usually announces the number of the hymn before the congregation starts singing it. In some services, hymns are accompanied on the piano and occasionally on the guitar, but usually tambourines supply the only musical accompaniment. Often the congregation's conception of the tune and the printed music used by the accompanist are at variance, which makes accompaniment difficult—there is a tendency for hymn tunes to acquire a calypso rhythm when sung by West Indians.

Hymns are sung complete, all verses in their proper order, and often the last verse is repeated two or three times, particularly if the hymn is used to introduce group prayer. In large meetings when there are insufficient hymn books to go round, and sometimes at smaller meetings, the leader reads each verse in a loud voice before the congregation sings it.

The chorus[11] is used to fill in gaps in the service when nothing else is

---

[11] See Appendix IX for examples.

happening, and to punctuate the various testimonies and sermons. Choruses consist of one or two verses repeated over and over again to the accompaniment of tambourines. Most of them are traditional in Pentecostal sects in Jamaica and elsewhere, but some have been composed by congregation leaders in England. Almost invariably choruses are sung from memory, though one sect, the Church of the Living God, has its own cyclostyled collection. Choruses are not announced by the leader as hymns are. A member (generally a nuclear one) starts singing and others join in. Often members rise to their feet and clap and dance while they sing, or keep time by rhythmic stamping.

Hymns and choruses provide the service with continuity and ensure that there is never a moment during which the congregation is not participating in some way. Enthusiasm created by preaching, testifying and ecstatic utterances is maintained by songs that embody the actual tenets of the saints' faith. Even more important, only in hymns and choruses does the congregation express itself uniformly as a group; testimonies, prayers, preaching are performed by individuals (albeit in a group situation) but in song the individual is submerged. I have shown that the congregation joins in the sung testimonies of individual members; the same happens with songs presented by a specially selected choir at large meetings. A 'choir' at such a meeting often comprises the whole of the host congregation.

Invocation Rituals

The avowed object of all services is the experiencing of the power of God by members. A successful service is one at which the Spirit is present and manifest. At most services the Holy Ghost is invoked in group prayers and invited to 'fill' the members, but sometimes a special ritual is performed besides; the City Mission always performs a special invocation ritual in large services. The leader stands before the congregation and recites the following formula (or one very like it), one sentence at a time, each sentence being repeated by the congregation:

> O Blessed Holy Ghost we welcome Thee,
> We welcome Thee in our singing,
> We welcome Thee in our prayers,
> We welcome Thee in our testimonies,
> We welcome Thee in the Message,
> We welcome Thee in our hearts
> O Blessed Holy Ghost
> We welcome Thee.

The Holy Ghost is invoked not at the beginning of the meeting, but only when most of those likely to attend have arrived and when members are beginning to show signs of enthusiasm. The invocation with its deafening responses very often itself stimulates the first outbreak of glossolalia. Probably because this rite is really impressive only in a well attended service, when the emotional impact of a hundred or more voices shouting the responses can be quite overwhelming, it is seldom used in the average small service attended by only twenty or thirty people. In small groups, enthusiasm does not appear to be so infectious and group prayer is a more efficient way of stimulating it. This seems to be especially so when a small group huddles in the front rows of seats in a large hall.

Bible Readings

At every meeting a passage is read from the Bible, sometimes by the leader, sometimes by a member invited to do so by the leader, or alternate verses may be read by the leader and the congregation.[12] The passage is usually a long one, a whole chapter, sometimes even two, and members follow it in their Bibles, interjecting if the leader makes mistakes or is defeated by unfamiliar words. At the end of the reading, the leader or the reader offers thanks to God for 'the reading of his wonderful Word'. As I have said, the leader and other preachers may hang their 'messages' on the passage read, but they are more likely to pick out one verse, which is used in the same way as 'Praise the Lord' to punctuate the exhortation. Where a sermon is more directly related to a passage read it is usually a narrative one such as a parable, or the story of Daniel in the Lion's den.

The passages chosen may come from any book of the Bible. I have recorded readings from all books except Leviticus and Proverbs during the two years of this study. There is a preference for the New Testament, although this is not so marked as might be expected among sects holding millennial doctrines. There is no doubt that some members derive aesthetic satisfaction from the dignified, archaic language of the King James Bible and choose passages because they like them rather than for their close bearing on doctrine. This, perhaps, accounts for the unflagging appeal of the Psalms, particularly the twenty-third: 'The Lord is my Shepherd, I shall not want . . .'

The Bible is the only basis for true doctrine and the sanction for all the rites performed in services. By reading it at meetings the congre-

[12] On two occasions I observed each member of the congregation read a verse.

gation affirms its loyalty to the revealed truth of Holy Writ, and to the Church, the community of worshippers whose existence is sanctioned by it.

3. *Intermittent Rituals*

In addition to regular rituals all sect congregations perform some rituals intermittently, or contingently. Intermittent ones are Communion and washing the feet of saints; contingent ones, funerary rites, weddings, healing and the dedication of children. Baptism and deliverance are sometimes contingent on a member asking to be baptised or delivered, but equally often the sect leader decides to perform the rite and then casts round for candidates. This is sometimes the case with healing, too; a leader asks those who require healing to come forward and they do so.

Communion

None of these sects celebrates Communion regularly. Regular celebration is considered a custom of the 'so-called churches' and without biblical sanction, but in fact many of them hold Communion services at approximately monthly intervals. The rite is commemorative rather than sacramental; they do not believe in transubstantiation nor do they think Communion necessary for salvation. It is a much less important rite than baptism.

There is some variation from sect to sect in the way the rite is performed. Some of them (Jesus Name sects) administer it as much as possible like a meal, with members sitting round a table. Others (Church of God) serve members in their seats, the bread and 'wine' being carried round by deacons. Usually these sects use little medicine glasses, whereas the Jesus Name ones use a common cup. Wine is never used for Communion, because of the powerful taboo against the use of alcohol. Various red or brown coloured liquids are substituted for it (on one occasion, even Coca Cola) but it is generally referred to as 'wine'.

All groups take the biblical phrase 'break bread' literally. An ordinary soft loaf, often a cottage loaf, is torn in half by the leader. Sometimes he tears it into small individual pieces but as often members pull off pieces themselves as it is carried round. Some groups deny strenuously that 'breaking bread' refers to anything but an ordinary meal, but their ritual remains the same.

Foot-Washing

Washing the feet of saints is practised by all the sects under consideration except the City Mission, in keeping with John xiii, 4–15, in which Christ's washing the feet of his disciples is described: 'If I then, your Lord and Master, have washed your feet, ye also ought to wash one another's feet. For I have given you an example that ye should do as I have done to you.'

The rite follows Communion, and I have the impression (though I have not heard it explicitly stated) that it is felt to be the more important of the two rites. This is partly because this rite marks off the Church of God and Jesus Name Sects from other Pentecostals and partly because of Christ's words to Peter who protested against having his feet washed: 'If I wash thee not, thou hast no part with me' (John xiii, 8).

For the rite the congregation splits into two groups—women at one end of the room, men at the other. Men never wash women's feet nor women men's. Each group has a basin or container of water and a towel. In a large congregation each group has more than one of these. Generally the leader starts by washing the feet of one male member of the congregation. The ceremony is completed when everyone present has had their feet washed and has washed the feet of someone else. The zealous wash the feet of more than one other member. In keeping with John xiii, 4–5, the member doing the washing girds himself with a towel to dry the feet he has washed. While this is going on, everyone sings a special chorus, 'We are washing one another's feet', and this is continued until all members have completed the rite and put on their shoes.

The rites of foot washing and Communion are special, almost festive occasions which help to stimulate the interest of members if it is flagging. Attendances at Communion are larger than at other services. Because other, non-Pentecostal churches perform the first rite somewhat differently and the second not at all, these rites serve to mark off the congregation from the world in a spectacular way.

Baptism

The rite of baptism has already been discussed as an induction rite which separates the full sect member from the 'world'. Here I will describe the ceremony itself.

It is held in a borrowed church, usually a Baptist one which has a tank. Neophytes sit in the front row of seats—men on one side, women on the other. Normally the women are dressed in white and men in black; the officiating leader also wears black, usually a robe. He wades into the tank and neophytes are brought to him in turn by sponsors. The neophyte does not have an individual sponsor, but two to four sponsors act for the whole group of neophytes. There is no special relationship between the neophytes and sponsors after the ceremony. The preacher announces the formula of baptism: 'I baptise you in the name of the Father, Son, and Holy Ghost' or 'of the Lord Jesus' or 'of Jesus' and topples the neophyte backwards so that momentarily he is entirely under the water. Sometimes before announcing the formula of baptism the leader asks the neophyte whether he appreciates the seriousness of the rite, and sometimes he 'gives' him a verse of Scripture.

The neophyte is helped out of the tank by one of the sponsors and goes out to put on his clothes. Candidates must behave as if they had passed through a significant and exhausting experience; they droop or stagger and sometimes indulge in mild ecstasy. After dressing they return, usually singly, and rejoin the congregation for the rest of the service.

The youngest child I have seen baptised was twelve years old. Although there is no hard and fast rule, a child younger than this is felt to be insufficiently mature to decide to follow Jesus. Nevertheless, children of members are not quite in the same category as the general body of the unsaved. In strict terms of the sects' ideology, a child who dies before being saved and baptised cannot enter heaven, but it is possible for a child to have been saved without anyone knowing about it and members give them the benefit of the doubt. On one occasion a City Mission leader expressed confidence that the soul of a member's dead baby (under a year old) was 'with Jesus'.

All sects except the Jesus Name ones accept the validity of baptism in other churches, provided that it has been by total immersion. No sect accepts baptism by what they contemptuously call 'sprinkling'. If pressed, members deny that those who have been baptised by 'sprinkling' can go to Heaven: '. . . John the Baptist didn't sprinkle Jesus, our Lord went right under the water.'

The anabaptist Jesus Name sects likewise insist on total-immersion baptism but do not consider it efficacious unless it is 'in Jesus' Name'. This means that the leader baptising the neophyte must announce: 'I baptise you in the Name of Jesus' as he thrusts him under the water.[13]

---

[13] One sect congregation in London rejects water baptism, holding that baptism in the Spirit is sufficient. This is the Gospel of Light and Truth Church of God mentioned in Appendix VIII at the end of Example 2.

The Gifts of the Spirit

The 'gifts of the Spirit' are wisdom, knowledge, faith-healing, working miracles, prophecy, discerning of spirits, tongues and the interpretation of tongues.[14] Of these, nuclear members have a near monopoly in healing, working miracles, prophecy, discerning of spirits and the interpretation of tongues, though instances of these manifestations do not even approach talking in tongues in frequency and importance in group rituals. This is brought out in Table 10:

TABLE 10

Relative Frequency of Gifts of the Spirit, City Mission, April 1961 to May 1962

Gift	Talking with Tongues	Healing	Prophecy	Interpretation of Tongues	Miracles other than Healing
No. of instances	35	13	1	1	0

Talking with tongues is relatively more frequent at services of the Church of the Living God; at every service someone talks with tongues. Healing is less frequent in this sect than it is in the City Mission. Other sect congregations probably fall somewhere between the two.

Gifts of the Spirit are not kept distinct in services. Often a member's performing a rite implies that he is using more than one gift of the Spirit: he who heals by commanding an 'unclean spirit' to leave a sick person is making use of the gift of discerning spirits as well as the gift of healing. Speaking in tongues, interpretation of tongues and prophecy likewise go together; a member who has spoken in tongues may interpret what he has said as a prophetic utterance.

Interpretation of tongues and prophecy are rituals whereby the congregation reaffirms its beliefs. They are neither instruments of government nor vehicles for innovation. They neither convey new information nor instruct saints to perform ritual acts they are not already performing. They are usually inspired by a scriptural text, such as 'the axe is laid to the root of the tree' or by a line from a

[14] I Cor. XII, 8–9: 'For to one is given by the Spirit the word of wisdom; to another the word of knowledge by the same Spirit; to another faith by the same Spirit; to another the gifts of healing by the same Spirit; to another the working of miracles; to another prophecy; to another discerning of spirits; to another divers kinds of tongues; to another the interpretation of tongues.'

hymn, such as 'watch and pray'. I have heard no prophecies that had any relevance to church government or to the practical day-to-day problems of the congregation.

The leader does not try to rule his congregation by uttering prophecies. He realises that prophecy is a two-edged tool: he is not the only one capable of prophesying and prophecies can disagree with one another. Only a leader with considerable personal charisma could employ prophecy in this way successfully, and none of the West Indian ones have enough.

Baptism in the Spirit

All the sects under consideration believe in the 'second baptism' which is also called the 'baptism of the Spirit', the 'baptism of fire' and the 'baptism of the Holy Ghost'. This is supposed to follow baptism in water and to be a special mark of divine favour. Sometimes, however, 'baptism of the Holy Ghost' precedes baptism in water, and indeed is an important factor in an individual's decision to be baptised in water. This has happened on two occasions when I have been present. Sect leaders generally do not seek to reconcile this with the usual doctrine, but say that 'the Holy Spirit moves as He will'.

Strictly speaking, a saint is baptised in the Spirit only once and baptism of the Spirit is distinct from the 'gifts of the Holy Spirit'. But although leaders make this distinction, it is made less clearly, if at all, by rank-and-file members, who may speak of being baptised in the Spirit several times. Baptism in the Spirit should, theoretically, always be accompanied by speaking in tongues. The Church of God of Prophecy's publication *Twenty-Nine Important Bible Truths* states that 'speaking in tongues as the Spirit gives utterance is the initial physical evidence of the baptism of the Holy Ghost. No one ever receives the Holy Ghost without speaking in tongues.' But here also official doctrine and members' practice are at variance; certainly some saints accept dancing, twitching, and lying or rolling on the ground as evidence of Spirit baptism as well. They also accept degrees of Spirit baptism from a 'real blessing' to 'just a touch'. Thus it can never be definitely determined whether a particular member has been baptised by the Holy Ghost or not. At nearly all services some member—usually several—ejaculate nonsense-syllables in the course of preaching, testifying, praying or while other people are doing these things. These ejaculations are felt to indicate that the member is especially inspired by God in the ritual act he is performing, or that he has been specially touched by someone else's performance.

Dedication of Infants

Although none of the sects under discussion practises infant baptism, babies are 'dedicated' to the service of Jesus. This takes place
towards the end of an ordinary service, is de-emphasised, and does
not resemble the rite of adult baptism. It is reasonable to suppose
that in a sect which baptises only adults, members are anxious about
the ritual relationship of their children to God and that the ceremony
of dedication has been instituted to allay this anxiety. This is one
aspect of the process by which a sect orientated towards recruitment
by voluntary association must make provisions for natural recruitment as well. Ideally a free association of saints held together only by
their desire to worship God, the church is forced to take account of,
and make provision for, other kinds of social bond. As well as being
Christians, members are parents. By this ritual an attempt is made to
integrate the family organisation of members with the organisation
of the religious group.

By the rite of infant dedication the child becomes a 'junior' member, an equivocal status intermediate between the 'saved' and the
'unsaved'. It is hoped that through attending Sunday School and
adult services, the child will be 'saved' and join the ranks of the
'saints', but as I have suggested, this is by no means certain.

Funerals

As most sect members are relatively young, funerals are rare.
Only one was celebrated in the City Mission during the two years of
this study, that of an infant. Most sects rely on the Church of England
or Baptist Church to perform the funeral service, and the sect takes
over the proceedings at the grave-side. Representatives, usually the
leaders, of many sects in the locality are present and these preach in
turn, so that the graveside ritual (while and after the grave is filled in)
may last for more than an hour. These sermons are very like those
preached in regular meetings, except that there are more references
to death and resurrection.

Weddings

Wedding ceremonies are also performed by a clergyman of one of
the established English churches, unless the sect has managed to
acquire a hall and register it for the celebration of marriages. At one
marriage ceremony I attended, in an Anglican church, a congregation
leader gave an address after the couple had been married by the
Church of England clergyman.

Because the wedding concerns many people who are not sect members, such as relatives of the bride and groom, friends, work-mates and perhaps the groom's English employer, the sect is forced to come to terms with the world. Prayers are said by some of the nuclear members, the congregation leader preaches, and the bride's parents also make speeches.

Deliverance and Healing

Towards the end of a service the leader may ask if anyone present needs healing or 'deliverance'. This is called an 'altar call' or 'coming to the throne of grace'.[15] Those who respond kneel at the front of the hall (immediately in front of the stage, if there is one) and the leader, some nuclear members and important people from other congregations pray over them, placing their hands on their shoulders or heads. The congregation prays at the same time. Sometimes all members of the congregation are called to the altar, whether they feel in special need of deliverance or not.

The 'deliverance' rite is identical in form with the rite whereby converts are accepted (on probation until they are baptised) into the congregation. Strictly speaking those who are saved, baptised in water and the 'Spirit', and are members of churches, are holy, free from sin, and therefore not in need of deliverance. At the time when Pentecostalism was growing and making large numbers of converts (early in this century) 'deliverance' must have been purely an induction rite. Today conversions are rare; the rite is still performed but it has changed its function. It is now a solidarity rite participated in by full members of the congregation who thereby re-live their conversion experience, behaving exactly as it is felt new converts should behave; they cry and grovel on the floor. It may still have some connection with induction since the unsaved may be led to follow their example, but there are seldom many unsaved people at sect services.

Closely associated with deliverance are healing rites. There are three of these: prayer (which has already been mentioned), the laying on of hands, and anointing with oil. Prayer may be used on its own and always accompanies the other two. Laying on of hands is part of the deliverance rite, but anointing with oil, the least frequently performed of the three rites, is only used in cases of physical sickness.

[15] This is a misnomer as there is no altar and these sects do not approve of altars. In front of the hall (on the stage if there is one) there is a lectern or a table which serves the same purpose. Hymn books, musical instruments and even the preacher's overcoat may be deposited on the table: it is in no sense holy.

Not all faith healing takes place in group situations; sometimes
members claim to have been healed simply by praying, without any
ritual having been performed over them.

Members accept both the popularly accepted explanation of illness
(infection and so forth) and their own magico-religious one. No
attempt is made to reconcile these or to work out the relationship
between them. Saints go to doctors and hospitals and take medicine
just as other people do, and at the same time seek to be healed by
faith. It is felt to be more holy, and to show more trust in God, to
seek to be healed by faith alone, and some members do this, but most
supplement conventional cures with religious ones or turn to religious
ones when no conventional cure is available or effective.

The sects believe that illnesses (though not perhaps all illnesses;
nobody is clear about this) are caused by spirit possession. Evil
spirits intervene in human affairs in other ways, by causing dissension
in the Church for example, but their most spectacular and most often
discussed activity is causing illness. The biblical sanction for healing
and casting out devils is provided by James v, 14: 'Is any sick among
you? Let him call for the elders of the church; and let them pray over
him, anointing him with oil in the name of the Lord: and the prayer
of faith shall save the sick and the Lord shall raise him up'; and by
Matthew x, 8: 'He said unto them: "Heal the sick, cleanse the lepers,
raise the dead, cast out devils: freely ye have received, freely give." '

As we have seen, it is felt that only some saints have the gifts of
'discerning spirits' and 'healing'. Nevertheless, most leaders try their
hand at it. The sick person kneels at the front of the room and the
healer or healers lay their hands on his head and command the 'unclean spirit' or 'spirit of sickness' to 'leave him, leave him in the name
of the Lord Jesus Christ'. This formula is repeated many times in the
course of long prayer. Sometimes no reference is made to spirits and
the formula repeated is 'Heal him, Lord! Heal him!' The rite of
anointing with oil is similar, except that olive oil is blessed and then
rubbed on the part of the body that is the seat of the sickness.
Leaders do not have oil to hand at every service, so anointings are
usually performed in response to a special request.

Most members believe that, for the rite to be successful, both the
person performing it and the person over whom it is performed must
have faith that a cure will be effected. Sometimes walking sticks are
taken from lame people or glasses from those with poor sight, since
their continuing to use them implies that they lack faith in the power
of God to heal.

In the case of really serious disabilities, probably even nuclear members are doubtful whether a cure will be effected; at least they express no disappointment when nothing happens. But I have neither recorded nor heard of healers refusing to perform the rite. A blind man twice submitted to healing rites at City Mission services I attended.

It was suggested by one leader that the presence of an unbeliever or a sinner in the congregation would prevent the Holy Ghost from healing, but others disagree and it does not appear to be generally believed.

Most of those seeking healing in sect services are suffering from minor ailments. I have attended no service in which the cure of a serious ailment was claimed. Members sometimes testify to having been cured of serious ailments in the West Indies before coming to England and there is a considerable folk-lore of astounding cures current in these sects: some, at least, of these cures derive from the various Pentecostal publications mentioned in the last chapter.

Probably at some time in their lives all members of a congregation make use of healing rituals, but some do so more frequently than others. Because they are often pregnant and anxious about their health, and because they have young children who are prone to the ailments of childhood, women are concerned in healing rites about three times as often as men. I received the impression that the healing rites of sects are more important to female members than to males; at least they talk about healing in their testimonies more often than men do.

VIII

INTERNAL ORGANISATION OF THE CONGREGATION

1. Members and non-Members

AMONG West Indian migrants in Britain there is no cultural or ideological barrier between members and non-members of Pentecostal sects. Almost all migrants, whether or not they are associated with Pentecostal or any other religious activity, accept the basic premises of Christianity as 'true doctrine'. Pentecostalism, which to the Englishman may seem exotic and eccentric, is close to the mainstream of the religious tradition in Jamaica, and is to the migrant a valid and socially acceptable form of religious expression. The West Indian crowd round a street-corner evangelist does not laugh or jeer; if anyone disagrees it will be seriously, over a point of doctrine.

The West Indian who does not take part in religious activity says that it is because he is not 'saved'; he is a 'sinner'. The real reason may often be an unwillingness to accept the taboos on drinking, smoking and extra-marital sexual relations imposed by Pentecostal and most nonconformist religious groups, but he does not question the description of these activities as sin. Sin is an estrangement from God, seen as a ritual shortcoming which is not necessarily socially reprehensible or a cause for guilt or embarrassment. The 'Christian' is one who takes ritual steps to approach God; the sinner one who does not.

Thus the Pentecostal proselytiser does not have to convince his listeners of the reality of sin or the utility of ritual means of overcoming it. Every working-class West Indian migrant is in a sense a potential convert, and although probably only about 5 per cent of West Indians in Britain are closely enough attached to sects to be considered members, at least twice as many are interested enough to attend services infrequently. I have seen some of these at services of several different sects; they seem to drift from congregation to congregation without becoming closely attached to any one.

A successful 'rally' and 'campaign' is attended by three or four or occasionally even ten times as many as attend regular services. Many of these extra people are invited members of other sects, but at least

3. Preaching

4. Washing the feet of the saints

5. Baptism

half of them are interested strangers belonging to no sect congregation.

It is from among interested non-members that the congregations hope to recruit. Some sects have a special name for them. The New Testament Church of God divides them into two categories, 'prospective members' and 'fellowshippers'. Table 11 gives the numbers of members, prospective members and fellowshippers in some New Testament Church of God congregations in London in April 1961. No figures were available for the other three London congregations of this sect, which are of more recent origin.

Congregations clearly vary considerably in the proportion of members to non-members. Although these figures refer specifically to the New Testament Church of God, my close study of the City Mission and the Church of the Living God suggests that there is a similar variation among the congregations of other sects. Not only do the different congregations of a sect vary in this but the same congregation varies from one period to another. (This is apart from the seasonal variations discussed in Chapter II.)

Demographic changes in the West Indian population in England are having a noticeable effect on congregation membership. Until the end of the 1950's the West Indian population was predominantly male, but since then an increasing number of women have arrived. In 1960 only about forty per cent of the average congregation were women; the percentage is now nearer sixty. It is likely that this process will continue until the sex ratio of 75:25, typical of the sects in Jamaica, is reached.[1]

Most of the recent female immigrants joining sect congregations are young and unmarried. When they marry, their husbands are very likely to be brought within the sect orbit as well, even if they do not actually become members. I have noticed this process beginning already within the City Mission. The sects' strict taboo on extra-marital and pre-marital sexual intercourse cannot fail to be to their advantage in this. Girls who are sect members would prove more difficult than the average to persuade into a temporary liaison, so they are more likely to marry the men they acquire. A man who is firmly and legally attached is more likely to be brought into the orbit of his wife's religious group than one lacking formal marital ties. As the economic causes of marital instability in Jamaica are absent in England I would expect the marriage-pattern of the immigrants to

---

[1] For this information I am obliged to Mr. Martin Ryder, who attended sect meetings in Jamaica on my behalf.

TABLE II

Members, Prospective Members and Fellowshippers in New Testament Church of God Congregations, 1960

Congregation	Members	Prospective	Fellowshippers	Totals	Percentage Members	Percentage Non-members	Totals
Brixton	57	30	100	187	30	70	100
Croydon	29	20	75	124	24	76	100
Hackney	14	20	35	69	20	80	100
Stoke Newington	59	30	150	239	25	75	100
Hammersmith	10	15	40	65	15	85	100
Kilburn	64	30	55	149	43	57	100
Totals	233	145	455	833	Average percentage 28	72	100

become increasingly like the local English pattern, becoming increasingly stable and long-lasting. In the short run this will be to the advantage of the sects, but as I suspect that the marital insecurity of women in Jamaica is one factor predisposing them towards sect membership, it may be to their disadvantage in the long run.

A 'member' of a sect congregation is one who has formally asked to become one and who has been formally accepted. Ideally there is no doubt about who is a member and who is not, but sometimes congregation leaders dispute over this, each claiming the allegiance of the same saint. Moreover, a saint claimed as a member by a congregation leader may deny that he is, saying that he is 'having Christian fellowship' with the congregation but is not a member of it. In addition a member may lose interest, progressively attending fewer and fewer services until he ultimately ceases attending at all. At this point the leader is unable and unwilling to say definitely whether he is a member or not.

Two categories of people are accepted as members, those who have already been 'saved' and baptised and those who have not hitherto been members of Pentecostal sects. As was seen in Chapter VII, all sects except the 'Jesus Name' ones accept as valid baptism in other churches provided it has been by total immersion.

Only adults and sub-adults can become full members of a sect congregation. The neophyte must be old enough to make the 'decision for Jesus'. Children, even very young ones, attend sect meetings, but they have no role in regular ritual. It is very unusual for a child to testify at a service, though this does happen sometimes. Not once have I seen a child indulge in ecstatic behaviour. At rallies and conventions the children of members are given a special part to play; they sing as a junior choir or form religious tableaux.[2] Practically all sect congregations run a Sunday School specially for the children, at which they are exhorted by adult leaders, learn their Bibles by playing Bible guessing-games and quizzes, and take part in a juvenile version of the adult service, being called upon to deliver short prayers and testimonies. Members regard this as a preparation for full participation when they are older.

Despite the ideological barrier to natural recruitment,[3] it is likely that growing up in a sect environment with parents who are members disposes the child towards becoming a member when old enough.

---

[2] On one occasion each child carried a placard bearing a letter of the alphabet to spell out the words, 'Jesus Saves'.
[3] See Chapter VII, pp. 72 ff.

It is impossible to say what proportion of children whose parents are saints become saints themselves, partly because few sects have been established in England long enough for children to have grown up here in a sect environment, and partly because the West Indian population of England is youthful and nearly all children of members are still very young.[4] Whether the children of saints become saints themselves when they grow up will depend on how thoroughly the West Indian population becomes assimilated in the next ten or fifteen years. Children growing up among English people, with English playmates who radiate the values of 'the world' as against those of the sect will be less likely to become sect members than those growing up in West Indian ghettoes who hear their parents' values challenged less often.

Pentecostal West Indians feel a special loyalty towards the sect in which they were baptised. Leaders of congregations who were baptised by the Kingston City Mission in Jamaica maintain close links with it in England even though they do not consider themselves members of it. Usually those baptised into one sect are more firmly attached to it than those who join it after being baptised into another one. To some extent undergoing baptism at the hands of a congregation leader indicates acceptance of his authority and seniority, so he therefore has more authority over people he has baptised himself than over people baptised by someone else.

2. *The Sect Nucleus*

A congregation meets on an average of five times a week, at least twice on Sundays, once on Saturdays, and twice on evenings during the week. Some members attend every one of these meetings as well as a few meetings of other congregations when they are invited to do so. But others attend at most one or two services a week and are more likely to stay at home when the weather is cold. The first category are referred to by the leader as 'faithful' members, or as 'our faithful few'. I am calling them 'nuclear' members.

The nucleus can be as few as five or six people in a small congregation or as many as thirty in a large one. It generally ranges from half to a quarter of the total membership. In the City Mission about twenty out of forty-five members could be considered nuclear.

The nucleus is not a group conscious of its own identity; nor is it

---

[4] Eighty per cent of the children of City Mission members in 1962 were under the age of seven. If a member has older children they are likely to have been left in Jamaica.

privileged in any obvious way. Nuclear members have more influence in the affairs of the congregation simply because they are always there when decisions are taken. Normally sect officers, Deacons, Elders and Sunday School teachers are chosen from among the nuclear members, but except in a very small congregation not all nuclear members are office-holders.

Over the years a few members are added to the nucleus and a few drift away because they have moved to another city, or have managed to save enough to return to the West Indies, or sometimes because of a quarrel with the leader. Three years after my first contact with the City Mission eighty per cent of the original nuclear members are still within the nucleus; this percentage would have been higher still had there not been a split in the sect in 1961.

Some nuclear members are sporadic in their attendance, coming to every meeting for a few months, abruptly ceasing to attend for a while and then, as abruptly, commencing to attend regularly once more. Some appear to lose interest in religion completely for a while and do not attend the services of any sect while absent from the congregation of which they are members; but others, while absent from its services, are flirting with other sects. Although other nuclear members suspect them of defection and sometimes publicly accuse them of it, criticism is silenced when they explain that they have been helping another 'worker for the Lord' establish his 'work'. Helping in the establishment of a new 'work' is a role especially suited to the requirements of the saint who now and again feels bored and restless in his congregation. It is a safety-valve which guards against its disintegration.

At any sect service most of those who preach or testify, pray aloud or indulge in ecstatic behaviour are nuclear members. At poorly attended services every nuclear member contributes in one or other of these ways, whereas only a few ordinary members do so. Often some of the nuclear members sit on the platform (if there is one) or behind a table with the leader. At the City Mission nearly all the nuclear members have conducted the service at some time during the last three years, but this congregation is atypical in that it has no one well-established leader in England.

Nuclear members probably consider themselves more holy, more closely in touch with God, than those who show less concentrated devotion. But this is never stated in so many words, and although they may seek to monopolise the ritual, the leader is careful to see that others have a chance of participating as well.

All nuclear members consider themselves to have been 'baptised in the Spirit', but so have most ordinary members as well. At meetings of the City Mission all but two nuclear members were observed to talk with tongues[5] or indulge in other ecstatic behaviour such as twitching at one or other of the 114 services I attended. Some nuclear members have behaved more or less ecstatically at every service I have attended, and the position in other groups appears to be the same.

In the City Mission only nuclear members prophesy. Likewise only nuclear members engage in faith-healing. Most healing rites are performed by the congregation leader, but nuclear members sometimes help him or perform healing rites on their own. Three or four of them stand round the sick person, lay their hands on him and pray loudly at the same time. The same happens when saints answer an 'altar call' and kneel at the front of the hall to ask God for 'deliverance', though then as many as ten nuclear members may pray and walk round the kneeling saints, laying their hands on each of them in turn.

Some nuclear members participate in healing and deliverance rites regularly; others never do. Although I have not heard it stated explicitly, it appears that only older nuclear members participate; it is felt inappropriate that young ones should do so.

The City Mission nucleus is atypical in that it is largely composed of people who knew one another in the West Indies before coming to England. Some of the older nuclear members have worked together in the City Mission ever since it parted from the Salvation Army in the early 1920's, and many of these were baptised by the senior bishop in Jamaica. In other sects there is little continuity in personnel between England and Jamaica; nuclear members are of heterogeneous derivation and were not members of the same congregation in the West Indies.

3. *Leaders of Pentecostal Sects*

Although anyone can lead a Pentecostal sect, saints feel that only an ordained minister should conduct marriage ceremonies, and that ordination confers divine authority to do so. Since most congregation leaders look forward to the day when they will own premises licensed for the solemnisation of marriage, they consider it necessary to be ordained. A few of them were ordained before coming to England, the others solve the problem in a variety of ways: one performed a ceremony of ordination on himself and then ordained his second-in-

[5] See examples in Appendix VI.

command. In the large sects the usual pattern is for the sect leader, the 'general overseer' in England, or the leader, 'overseer' of one of the administrative districts into which they divide England, to ordain congregation leaders. I have the impression, though it is never stated explicitly, that sect leaders are somewhat reluctant to do this for fear of the fissive effects of giving a congregation leader too much prestige. Where ordination involves the transmission of authority to perform ritual from a sect leader to one of his congregation leaders, or from a sect leader to the leader of another sect, which occurs very rarely, then the ceremony consists of laying on of hands, or laying on of hands and anointing with oil. I gather that when God ordains a leader directly, in a vision, these ceremonies are unnecessary.

Not all congregation leaders are ordained; some congregations are led by 'Elders'. The City Mission has not, in eight years of its existence in England, had an ordained minister permanently resident here, though bishops from the West Indies and the United States have visited the English congregations from time to time.

Just as not all congregations are led by ordained ministers, so not all sect organisations are led by bishops. All the large, internationally organised sects have at least one bishop in England, but few of the smaller ones do. This is not on account of any difficulty in assuming the title of bishop; some of those in England have simply enthroned themselves, or, as they see it, been enthroned directly by God. Perhaps the leaders of very small sects feel that it would be slightly ridiculous to call themselves 'bishops', though some of them do. These are mainly Jesus Name, Apostolic groups who believe that their leaders are the heirs of the apostles and should, therefore, be called bishops.[6]

Perhaps if there had been more contact between the growing assemblies in England and the well-established ones in the United States during the early 1950's, United States bishops would have visited England to enthrone local ones, but it was only in the late 1950's that they began visiting England, and by then all the large sects were well established.

West Indian Pentecostal clergy seldom wear clerical garb, though most ordained ministers own a set. Bishops have colourful robes

---

[6] Certain biblical texts can be interpreted as meaning that only a married man can be a bishop. This may deter some of the younger, unmarried leaders from assuming the title.

consisting of a garment like a graduate gown and a stole;[7] but they wear them only on very special occasions, probably no more than twice or three times a year.

Normally the ordained congregation leader dresses like other saints, without even a clerical collar. Members address him more often as 'Brother' than as 'Reverend' or 'Minister', and some ordained leaders are commonly addressed and referred to as 'Elder'. The leader is not offended by this, but he is likely to be offended if a white clergyman fails to address him or refer to him as 'the Reverend', 'Pastor', or 'Bishop', as this is felt to imply a refusal to recognise the validity of Pentecostal, or more especially West Indian Pentecostal Holy Orders.

It seems that being led by an ordained minister or bishop is more important in a congregation's relations with other congregations and with non-West Indian churches than it is in its own internal organisation. Congregations led by ordained ministers or bishops are no less prone to fission than those led by people laying no claim to holy orders.[8] The authority of the congregation leader in his own congregation is augmented very little by his ordination. It is mainly an announcement of his claim to treat as an equal with the leaders of other sects. He generally wears clerical dress at a service only when members of other sects are present at it.

[7] As far as I know, only one congregation leader who does not claim to be a bishop has robes.

[8] One sect of the Church of God in Christ led by a bishop has suffered almost as many splits as the rest put together.

IX

ECONOMIC PROBLEMS

1. *Larger Sects*

THE economic problems of the large, internationally organised sects are very different from those of the many much smaller ones, and their financial arrangements are consequently different. However, as far as I have been able to discover, none of the international sects receives financial assistance from the United States. Though members of smaller sects often accuse them of doing so, the leaders deny this vigorously, and, in the absence of evidence to the contrary, I see no reason to disbelieve them. Sects in America do give money for missionary enterprises but the congregations in England are not felt to qualify as such, regardless of the fact that they may think of themselves as missions.

Not all the large sects keep strict accounts. Some of them have no bank account distinct from that of the leader and reports of income and expenditure are not made at meetings.[1] A congregation's economic problem cannot always be clearly separated from the private economic problems of the congregation leader, as it is he who feels himself ultimately responsible for the 'work of God'. Many leaders do not distinguish their own income from the income of the church in any very precise way. I am satisfied that very few leaders gain by this; indeed most of them lose by it. The success of the church is their personal success and they frequently have to pay expenses out of their own pockets if attendance at services is small and there is little money in the plate. Many leaders take it for granted that they should earn money themselves to finance special schemes such as a four-day Easter campaign or a trip to visit another congregation in a distant city. Believing that 'God will find a way', that fervent prayer ensures success, many of them shoulder debts with no guarantee that the congregation's contributions will be sufficient to meet them.

The larger, multi-congregational sects raise much of their income by tithing. The Church of God of Prophecy, the New Testament Church of God and the Church of God in Christ all require their

---

[1] Disgruntled members sometimes complain about this and it can be one of the issues over which congregations split.

members to pay a tenth of their incomes to the church.[2] This is usually interpreted as a tenth of gross income, not a tenth of what remains after essential expenses such as food, rent and clothing have been deducted. It is very difficult to find out whether members of a congregation really do pay their tithes, but from the known incomes of some sect congregations it is reasonable to conclude that most of them do. A member who refuses can be and often is 'disfellowshipped'. Even allowing for the high rate of unemployment among unskilled West Indians and their low earning power, the tithes of a well-established congregation provide a regular income on which the congregation leader can count when planning expenditure. If each member contributes about ten shillings per week throughout the year, a nuclear membership of forty would bring in about £1,000. Added to this are 'free-will offerings', comprising the gifts of members and the collections taken up at services.

The 1960–1 income of a London congregation of the New Testament Church of God which claimed fifty-nine members in 1961 consisted of £900 from tithes and £200 from free-will offerings, making a total of £1,100.[3] This is probably typical of large congregations of the international sects. A third (three out of nine) of the London congregations of the New Testament Church of God had more than fifty members and probably therefore an income of about £1,000 a year. This is apart from the proceeds of special fund-raising projects to buy church buildings.

For the reasons discussed in Chapter III nearly all sects in England aspire to buy their own hall one day. Some of them have raised a great deal of money for this purpose and are able to pay a deposit as soon as they can find a suitable building.[4] But halls are not easy to find close to members' homes, and the fact that half a dozen sects may be competing to buy halls in the same district makes it no easier. They compete with one another for accommodation just as they do for members and it has been suggested to me by congregation leaders

[2] The late Bishop Johnson of the Church of the Lord Jesus Christ of the Apostolic Faith said: 'If you do not give God the tenth of all your income you will be cursed with a curse, according to Mal. iii, 9, op. cit., p. 12. Tithing is as much a ritual as an economic activity. Like testifying, washing the feet of saints or talking with tongues, it is, in itself, pleasing to God. Members pay tithes because they believe strict adherence to biblical injunctions essential to their salvation, rather than because they recognise tithing as the most convenient way of financing the congregation.

[3] From a report read at a meeting 3 April 1961.

[4] By the middle of 1961 the City Mission had raised £2,600. A small, one-congregation sect had raised £1,100.

that this fierce competition has inflated the prices of halls. This may well be so.

I know of no sect (apart from the City Mission) which has been able to raise the full purchase price of a hall.[5] This makes it necessary for them to seek loans or mortages. But mortgage companies, doubting their ability to repay, are generally reluctant to lend money to people in unskilled, poorly paid occupations, and most congregation leaders are in this category.

But the zeal of the saints can overcome even obstacles as great as this. If the finance company will not accept one member as guarantor of the loan, then two or more members jointly undertake responsibility for repayment. This happened in 1962 when the City Mission bought a building in East London as its headquarters in Britain.

Sometimes the title-deeds of a building bought in this way bear the name of the sect, but as often it may bear those of the guarantors of the loan. The histories of the larger of these sects in the United States and of native English Pentecostal sects in Britain suggest that although the acquisition of property by sect congregations solves immediate problems of accommodation it lays up a legacy of trouble for the future.[6] Sects that own nothing can split relatively painlessly and with a minimum of rancour, but when once they own property every split raises the question of its ownership and may lead to undignified, costly and bitterly contested law-suits.[7] That the sects under discussion will have these troubles in future is indicated by the bitterness with which they squabble over the right to use rented halls at present. On one occasion a sect leader padlocked a hall against a congregation in revolt; they smashed the padlock with a sledgehammer and there has been talk of legal action on both sides.

Before a congregation can attempt to buy a hall it must have a

---

[5] Since this was written the New Testament Church of God has bought property in London and Birmingham. The most recent purchase (1964) was a former Methodist church in Willesden, for which about £10,000 was paid. The central organisation in the United States made a grant towards this and the members in England raised the balance. By mid-1964 none of the other sect organisations (with the exception of the City Mission) had been able to buy property.

[6] Elim and Bible Pattern, whose fission is discussed in Appendix III, are at present engaged in a dispute over the ownership of property. Elim stands to win, as most property appears to be vested in the Elim Church; this has been, and is, one of the articles of Elim's constitution. I gather that disputes over property have also accompanied a recent fission of the Exclusive Brethren (the less liberal branch of the Plymouth Brethren); it is not a feature of Pentecostal sects alone.

[7] The split in the Church of God between 1923 and 1927 is described in Appendix II. In England the Elim Church evicted Bible Pattern followers from their churches.

fairly large sum of money (between £1,000 and £3,000) as a deposit. No leader or individual member ever has as much as this, so ways must be found of raising it. This can be done by a direct appeal to members to give or lend their savings, by holding entertainments at which collections are taken up, by collections made by members among non-members, English as well as West Indian, at their place of work, and, rarely, by seeking help from members and friends in the West Indies. The City Mission used all these methods in raising its 'building fund', but not all sects are so enterprising.

Few saints have large amounts of capital saved. What they have is usually sent back to the West Indies for the support of children and other relatives. Also many of them are buying the houses in which they live and have little over from their week's earnings after making mortgage repayments. There may be relatives out of work to be helped as well. Despite such commitments and the saints' very low earning power, anything up to £1,000 may be raised in gifts and loans from members. Sometimes a member pledges a half of his earnings or his whole pay-packet for a week or fortnight. A maximum of fifty members of the sect can be involved in this. Usually it tends to be twenty or thirty, about half of whom are women, who earn less than the men. Raising a building fund stretches the financial resources of members to the limit.

Members demonstrate their zeal by the scale of their gifts, and even those who cannot afford a handsome gift are shamed into giving one. If a member stands up in a meeting and publicly pledges a proportion of his wages, others nearly always follow suit. Those who have no money at all, often because they are unemployed, feel obliged to explain this publicly, sometimes adding a promise to contribute if and when they find employment. As all members know one another intimately it is difficult for one of them to plead poverty unless he is indeed practically destitute. A refusal to contribute, of which I have recorded no instances, would indicate that the member lacked zeal for the work of God, that he was attached to the 'things of the world'. There are very powerful social pressures bearing on members to contribute as much as they possibly can. Equally, facing the common problem of raising money for a common purpose is a powerful cohesive force in the congregation.

A favourite fund-raising technique is the 'rally'. Rallies are sometimes held without the object of raising funds, but most of them (about 60 per cent of those I have attended) have this as an object. Nuclear members organise themselves to entertain peripheral members, members of other congregations and non-Pentecostal West Indians. Entertainment includes dramatic productions, songs and recitations by individuals, songs by the 'choir', and songs and recitations by members' children. All these items naturally have a strongly religious flavour.

Sometimes an element of competition is introduced by dividing members into two or four groups which perform separately. The groups are named (on one occasion after four of the tribes of Israel) and those present are urged to support the group of their choice by giving generously when it performs. The winning group is the one which collects the most money. Such competitions generate great excitement and quite large sums are collected in this way; the most collected by a 'tribe' during the City Mission's Rally of the Tribes of Israel was just under £40 and the least just over £15. After each item collectors go round the congregation; few give less than a shilling and many give pound notes. After each collection the money is counted and the totals for each group are announced.

Collections at rallies are made after solo hymns and recitations as well. Particularly melodious or stirring contributions provoke demands for an encore, but before these are complied with the congregation must pay for it! If the collection is not big enough the performer may refuse to give his encore until the plate is passed round again.

The congregation at a rally is made up of members of the congregation holding it, their friends and neighbours, and members of other sects who have been specially invited. Some other sect congregations come in force, others send a few representatives, usually including their leader, to give moral if not financial support. This makes for a degree of financial interdependence among the various sects. A congregation that does not attend another's rally when invited to do so cannot expect support from that quarter when it holds its own rally.

As well as giving generously at rallies, each member of the congregation is expected to raise money on his own account. The City Mission issued members and well-wishers with printed cards on which contributions of 6d., 1s., 2s., 2s. 6d., 5s., 10s., and £1 could be recorded. These provided proof of the bona fides of the member asking for contributions as well as a record of the amount he collected. As far as I know, no other sect has used this method.

As gambling is regarded as sinful by all the sects under discussion, they are prevented from holding raffles, which might otherwise be very profitable. Nor have I heard of their holding fêtes or jumble sales, the most usual forms of fund-raising among English organisations. This is probably because West Indian households have not been established long enough to contain the kind of unwanted bric-à-brac sold at jumble sales, but it is also difficult to find somewhere to hold such a function. Most West Indians would feel that England is much too cold for them to be held out of doors.[8]

A very few congregations (only four to my knowledge) do not engage in money-raising activities. Members of these congregations believe that since there is no biblical authority for it, it must be against the will of God. No collection is taken up at services; a plate stands on a table and members are expected to put their contributions on it as inconspicuously as possible after the service has ended. Needless to say, none of these congregations aspires to buying a building of its own.

2. *Small Sects*

The small sect of one or two congregations is financially in a very different position from the large ones. Often the congregation is so small (perhaps no more than ten) that if members did pay tithes they would yield very little. But very few of them do; those who do not do so consider it to be unscriptural,[9] and deprecate 'turning God's house into a money-making business'. Some of them have split from the larger sects over the issue of tithing.

A very small sect cannot make a success of tithing, as the pastor cannot afford to 'disfellowship' members who do not pay—he has too few of them. Members, knowing this, are not likely to be impressed by threats of disfellowshipment. The typical small-sect congregation consists of two or three family groups of husband, wife and children, and a handful of people without close kin in England who very often rent rooms from one or other of the families. If the leader, who is seldom a member of one of the families, 'disfellowships' a member it means that his spouse and children leave too, often taking the lodger with them. So many people leave that the sect, in reality, splits: the

---

[8] It is worth noting in this context that, despite the strong tradition of peasant marketing in the West Indies, there are practically no West Indian street-traders in England. In Portobello Road market, for example, even West Indian foodstuffs are sold by Englishmen.

[9] The biblical argument against tithing is as follows: although tithes are mentioned in the Old Testament this was a law applicable only until the arrival of Christ. Tithes, like the food-taboos of the Jewish Law, have no place in the 'dispensation of Grace' under which we are now living.

withdrawal of one family is no very serious matter for a large congregation, but it can kill a very small one, as those remaining may be
too few to afford the rent of the room or hall in which the group
meets.

Generally the small sect can derive a larger income from free-will
offerings than it can from tithes. As nearly every member holds some
office or title in the congregation, everybody feels responsible for its
success and gives generously, probably more than the tenth required
by tithing sects. At the inaugural business-meeting of one small sect
congregation in South London in 1961, members were called upon
in turn to declare how much they would be able to contribute. Not
one of the six male members promised less than £1 per week and
three of them promised £3. All of them were unskilled workers and
none could have been earning more than £12 per week. I was unable
to find out how many of them made good their promises and for how
long their good intentions lasted, but their zeal was at least sufficient
to get the sect started and it was still operating two years later.

Whereas the large, multi-congregational sect can count on a fairly
steady income and can plan in terms of it, the small one often incurs
expenses without anyone having the slightest idea of how they will
be met. When bills come in members offer prayers at a service and
very often the feeling of crisis and urgency this generates prompts
them to make contributions. The collection of the sum required is
hailed by all as a direct intervention of God in answer to prayer.
Group prayer can be a very efficient mechanism for overcoming
financial obstacles; furthermore, participation in it reinforces the
faith of members in the beliefs they all share and re-emphasises the
importance of their church as a group. Every obstacle overcome in
this way strengthens the church.

The small sects, and in theory at least the larger ones as well,
have no clearly thought-out financial policy. 'God will provide' is a
cornerstone of West Indian Pentecostal belief. Leaders who express
anxiety about finance or appear to take too much care in planning it
are likely to be criticised for lack of faith. Any sect activity must be
'the work of God', not of man; it must wait on 'the moving of the
Spirit'. This point of view seriously inhibits planning of any kind,
and goes a long way towards explaining the absence of coherent
objects and of the financial planning these require, always excepting
the purchase of buildings. But in addition no sect leaders come from
the kind of background that would give them financial experience.
The typical small sect is run like a Jamaican peasant holding; im-

mediate economic crises are met as they arise, from day to day and
from week to week. Paradoxically, all saints with whom I have discussed the problem agree that the work of God—the preaching of the
Word to an increasing number of lukewarm believers and unbelievers—would benefit from more efficient planning.

3. *Collections and their Expenditure*

Sects of all sizes take up collections at services. The collection
made at a service is usually earmarked in advance to pay the rent of
the hall in which the group meets. If, as sometimes happens, the
amount collected is insufficient for this purpose, the deacons may be
asked by the leader to take their plates round again. Sometimes the
leader announces how much the collection is short of the required
amount and asks members to make it up, perhaps suggesting how
much each should contribute to achieve this.

At all services of Father, Son and Holy Ghost sects the collection
is solemnly dedicated to the work of God before it is counted. One of
the two members who have taken round the plates is asked to do this
by the leader. The dedication commences with a long prayer, often
on a theme or biblical text already mentioned in the service, and con-
cludes with a special formula:

> This free-will offering is sealed and signed,
> Sealed by the Father,
> Sealed by the Son,
> Sealed by the Holy Ghost,
> Sealed and signed.

The congregation repeats each line after the person performing the
dedication. The offering remains in the plates until the end of the
service when it is counted by the leader, perhaps assisted by one of
the deacons, and put in an envelope. At meetings of the City Mission
the sum is then entered in a note-book, but this does not always
happen in other sects, though the leader may make a record of it
afterwards. The Jesus Name sects do not perform a dedication ritual
and some of them, as I have said, do not formally take up a collection
at all.

Money collected at a service is believed to be especially dedicated
to God's work and after the rent for the hall has been paid it has to be
decided for what purpose the surplus (if any) is to be used. Theoretically there is no distinction between the private affairs of members
and the work of God. They are supposed to be engaged on God's

work all the time; they work to support themselves to serve God, they marry and rear families to serve God, they migrated from the West Indies to serve God. The Church composed of saints is thought of as the 'Bride of Christ' and so, in a sense, the welfare of members is God's work. Because members exist only to serve God there can be no conflict between the interests of members and those of the church.

This is the theoretical standpoint of saints, but there is often conflict within congregations over what constitutes God's work and what does not. When the City Mission had raised enough money for a deposit on a building, some members felt that a hall should be purchased, whereas others supported the purchase of a house which, while having a room large enough for services, would also provide accommodation for members. In general those who looked forward to solving their accommodation problems in this way supported the second plan and those who had already solved them by buying houses opposed it.

At any time in any congregation there are members who feel that their private schemes merit financing by the church. Some of these are accepted and some rejected. A solution may be found by taking up special collections among members for special projects. In this way presents of money called 'love offerings' are raised to help finance the travels of leaders abroad or to help the few members who leave to return home to the Caribbean.

If it is difficult to distinguish the private affairs of members from the work of God; it is even more difficult to distinguish the private life of the leader, ordained or unordained, from his public role as 'servant of God'. It is agreed to be appropriate that a leader should receive some financial assistance from the church, but congregations vary a great deal in the amount of help they give him. It may vary all the way from a salary sufficient to support him to a small contribution towards the expenses he incurs in transacting church business. In very small sects arrangements tend to be informal and the leader simply uses what is left of the offerings after the rent for the hall has been paid. Only once have I heard a leader make specific demands on his congregation, enumerating the expenses he incurred in ministering to them and suggesting that the church should pay them.

Practically all congregation leaders have secular jobs and as a group they appear to be reliable, consistent workers. That they hold the same job for a long time is probably due to the fact that they are tied to a particular district by their congregations and so cannot move about as much as many migrants do. Few of those with whom

I have discussed the matter expect to give up work in the future to live on stipends paid by their congregations. Indeed there can be no economic advantage in being a full-time, paid congregation leader; few congregations could afford to pay their leader as much as he could earn even in unskilled work.

Very seldom, then, has the salary of the leader to be met out of the congregation's income, nor does it often make an appreciable contribution to his living expenses. If he has a car, and as far as I know only two in London do, then he may receive some help in meeting its running expenses. The congregation may also pay his fares if he has to travel to another city to preach the gospel or to treat with other West Indian religious leaders.

4. *Other Items*

Pentecostal sects have few other running expenses. Little equipment is needed for the satisfactory performance of sect rituals and none of it is very costly. Fifty hymn books (Sankey's *Sacred Songs and Solos* or the *Redemption Hymnal* published by the Elim Church), half a dozen tambourines, a Communion set consisting of small glasses in a wooden stand or, alternatively one large glass, two plastic or enamel bowls and two towels for use in the rite of washing the feet of saints,[10] complete the list of essential equipment. Musical instruments other than tambourines are always the private property of members; I have recorded the use of guitars, clarinets, violins and cymbals at services, but at most of them only tambourines are used. Bowls and towels for foot-washing are also sometimes the property of individual members and are otherwise used for ordinary domestic purposes. Foot-washing is not performed very often, perhaps an average of five or six times a year, so it is not always felt worth while to invest in bowls and towels specially for the purpose. The cost of this equipment is little more than ten pounds (fifty Sankey hymn books cost only £6 5s. retail and a tambourine can be bought for less than £1).

Nearly all sects circulate some kind of 'news-letter', usually cyclostyled, at monthly, quarterly or irregular intervals. These are generally typed by the leader and cyclostyled commercially. I have seen these distributed at services on three occasions.

All sect congregations have periodic campaigns and conventions

---

[10] This rite is performed by all the sects under discussion except the City Mission. It should, according to their official doctrines, be performed at least once a year. In all of them it is the final part of the Communion rite.

which they advertise by handbills posted to members, sympathisers and the leaders of some other congregations. These are printed commercially and constitute the sect's only attempt at advertising itself, apart from outdoor meetings. No sect advertises in the newspapers. It is doubtful if the average congregation spends more than a pound a week on printing; many of them spend much less.

X

CONTACT BETWEEN WEST INDIANS AND ENGLISH RELIGIOUS GROUPS

1. *The Larger Denominations*

CLERGYMEN in England often complain that West Indians show no interest in English churches. Some are puzzled by this, as they have been told by clergymen who have worked in the West Indies that the people there are very religious and attend church assiduously. Many of them feel that they have fallen down on the job of assimilating the migrants into native English congregations, but at the same time they are at a loss to know how they should go about it.

That very few West Indians do attend English churches is borne out by a brief survey I conducted in 1960.[1] This was intended to provide background to the study of West Indian Pentecostal sects in which I was mainly interested, rather than give a complete picture of West Indian participation in English religious groups. As the issue was peripheral to the main study I did not attempt to survey all English denominations but chose three of them, the Church of England, the Congregationalists and the Seventh Day Adventists.

I chose the Church of England because Jamaican census returns suggest that many Jamaicans belong to it (28·3 per cent in the 1943 census), the Congregationalists because it is a small denomination in Jamaica (1·7 per cent in 1943) and it seemed reasonable to suppose that if Jamaican patterns of Church membership were being followed in England the difference between these two denominations would be readily apparent. It turned out that there was no marked difference between the numbers attending Church of England and Congregationalist churches when allowances are made for the much greater number of Church of England churches available for migrants to attend, so it appears that migrants do not attend churches in England in the same proportions as they did in Jamaica.

I chose the Seventh Day Adventists because they proselytise very

[1] Since then a more detailed investigation has been conducted by the Rev. Clifford Hill into the participation of West Indians in London churches. See Clifford S. Hill: *West Indian Migrants and the London Churches*, London, Oxford University Press for the Institute of Race Relations, 1963. His conclusions agree with mine.

actively and I suspected that proselytisation was an important factor in West Indian church attendance. A closer study of Seventh Day Adventist congregations bore out this assumtpion.

No attempt was made to sample congregations within the three churches chosen; but on the basis of information gathered by the Institute of Race Relations in the course of a survey of West Indian settlement in England[2] I sent questionnaires to all clergymen of these churches in areas having dense West Indian populations. Clergymen in London were not sent questionnaires, but were interviewed instead. I hoped that this more personal contact with members of the clergy would assist me in interpreting the questionnaire material from other towns.

Clergymen were asked in the questionnaire:

1. The average attendance at services in their churches;
2. The average West Indian attendance;
3. The number of faithful West Indian members;
4. Whether any West Indians held office in the church;
5. Whether they knew of any other churches in the district with West Indian members.

Of ninety-one questionnaires sent out, fifty-two were returned. Of these thirty-eight reported some West Indian members, though 'some' often amounted to only one. It is likely that a large proportion of those clergymen who failed to return the questionnaire had no West Indian members at all. Talking to clergymen in London I found that those who had West Indian members were interested in them and anxious to co-operate in the survey, whereas those who had none were less interested. As I see no reason why clergy in other cities should react differently from those in London, lack of interest revealed in failure to complete the questionnaire must very often have indicated the absence of West Indian members. Had a larger number of questionnaires been returned it is likely that the total picture would have been of less West Indian participation rather than of more.

A much higher proportion of Seventh Day Adventist clergymen returned the questionnaire than Church of England and Congregationalist ones. Usually there was only one Seventh Day Adventist Church in each town whereas there were several of the other two denominations. Figures for Seventh Day Adventists are therefore totals for a town, whereas those for the other two denominations

---

[2] *Coloured Immigrants in Britain*, London, Oxford University Press for the Institute of Race Relations, 1960.

are an unknown part of the totals. Nevertheless, apart from West Indian Pentecostal sects, few other churches were reported in Question 5 as having West Indian members. Table 12 shows that even if the numbers attending Congregationalist and Church of England

TABLE 12

West Indian Membership of Selected English Congregations, 1961

Town	Church of of England		Congregationalists		7th Day Adventists	
	Number	Per cent of Congregation	Number	Per cent of Congregation	Number	Per cent of Congregation
Bedford	4	1	5	2·5	150	60
Birmingham	10	3·2	0	0	150	60
Bristol	—	—	2	2·5	—	—
Coventry	8	3·2	—	—	7	11
Derby	—	—	—	—	18	33
Gloucester	6	2	0	0	10	20
Huddersfield	5	2·5	—	—	30	75
Ipswich	—	—	—	—	9	11
Leeds	—	—	41	2·3	14	18
Leicester	22	1·9	—	—	—	—
Liverpool	14	3·5	1	2	3	6
London	69	6·3	32	?	183	70
Luton	4	1	12	4	50	83
Manchester	20	10	3	2·5	—	—
Nottingham	—	—	4	2	—	—
Oxford	—	—	—	—	4	10
Reading	—	—	—	—	8	13
Sheffield	4	3·5	—	—	—	—
Slough	—	—	—	—	23	35
Southampton	—	—	—	—	2	5
Total	148	3·6	100	1·78	511	32

churches in a town were five times those reported, they would still be a remarkably small part of the total West Indian populations given in Table 13. Even if some congregations with West Indian members were missed in the survey the conclusion that immigrants do not attend Congregationalist and Church of England churches would

TABLE 13

*Estimated West Indian Populations of Selected
English Towns, 1958**

Town	West Indian Population
Bedford	400
Birmingham	20,000
Bristol	2,000
Coventry	400
Derby	1,000
Gloucester	600
Huddersfield	2,000
Ipswich	?
Leeds	2,000
Leicester	400
Liverpool	1,000
London	40,000
Luton	300
Manchester	4,500
Nottingham	3,000
Oxford	250
Reading	350
Sheffield	3,000
Slough	?
Southampton	750

* Derived from *Coloured Immigrants in Britain*, Oxford University Press for the Institute of Race Relations, 1960.

still be inescapable. As no Methodists, Presbyterians or Baptists were mentioned by the clergymen who replied as having a large West Indian following, this conclusion is almost certainly true of them as well. (The Seventh Day Adventists, who do have a large West Indian following, will be discussed in the next section.)

Most clergymen with whom I have discussed the subject believe the immigrant notices that church-going is not nearly so common in England as it is in the West Indies, and that in England one can be 'respectable' without attending church; they copy English social behaviour and stay away. F. M. Henriques emphasies the role of the larger churches, especially the Church of England and the Baptists, in cementing social solidarity in Jamaica. He says:

. . . organised religion in the form of the orthodox churches does, however, serve an extremely important social end. It was suggested earlier that the market acts as a binding force in society. A church has a similar function. Here the upper and middle-class men and women meet not only each other but members of the lower classes as well. The orthodox churches are a powerful factor making for solidarity.[3]

This would hardly be true of modern England. Although the Church of England has members in all social classes, its constituent congregations do not, at least not in big cities;[4] different churches in different parishes are patronised by different social classes. The Baptists, who in Jamaica have members in all social classes, tend to be a working-class and lower middle-class church in England and are thus hardly in a position to cement social solidarity. Over and above this, too few people in England attend church regularly for church-going to be a society-wide demonstration of solidarity.[5]

Possibly West Indians are recognising that churches in England and Jamaica have different social functions when they complain that English churches are 'cold'. This must be particularly noticeable to migrants from rural areas, where the function of the church in cementing solidarity tends to be most pronounced.

Although the different functions of churches in England and Jamaica go a long way towards explaining the West Indian's failure to attend church in England, I do not think this is a full explanation. If churches in England were as well integrated with society as they are in Jamaica it is still doubtful whether immigrants would attend them. Does the migrant want to identify with English society and celebrate his feelings of solidarity with it in church services? I do not think he does. He comes to England to make money, to win a better standard of living for himself and his dependants back home. He regards himself as a temporary migrant. England is not 'home' to him and he does not seek to sink roots in English society. In fact he may deliberately avoid commitment to it, as this might make it more difficult for him to return home.

Of course few migrants do, in fact, achieve their goal of returning home prosperous after a few years' work in England. Typically one year becomes five, and five years ten. Housing difficulties force them to buy houses on mortgages and their houses tie them to England. Despairing of reunion with their families in the West Indies, they

---

[3] F. M. Henriques: *Family and Colour in Jamaica*, p. 76.

[4] This would be less applicable to rural areas.

[5] It may however reinforce the solidarity of minorities. Both Irish and Jewish minorities differ from the general population in religion and by going to church or synagogue celebrate their solidarity. In this they resemble the members of West Indian sects.

send for dependants and relatives one by one as they can afford the passage-money; and so the family becomes established in England. Children go to school in England, make English friends and come to accept English patterns of social behaviour. One has only to watch West Indian and English children playing together in the streets to realise what close ties with England are being forged, and how much more difficult it becomes for the migrant family to return home, with every year it stays in England.[6]

If the migrant ever comes to accept that he is in England for good, and very few of those I know do, his pattern of adjustment to English society has by this time hardened, has become a habit. He has become used to living on its fringes and participating no more than is necessary to make a living. During his first few years in England he did not want to identify with English society; after being settled for many years he is no longer able to do so.

If this argument is correct, one would not expect the migrant to participate in church services out of a wish to identify with English society, but rather that if he joins any religious group, he will join one which, far from identifying with society-at-large, emphasises its divorce from it. This is precisely the satisfaction the West Indian derives from belonging to a Pentecostal religious sect. But there are demographic as well as sociological factors favouring this choice. Although 54 per cent of the population of Jamaica are Baptist or Church of England according to the 1943 census, it is doubtful whether nearly as high a percentage of those coming to England are members of these denominations.

Most of the migrants are unskilled or semi-skilled workers, poor and ill-educated; precisely those who would be likely to follow a Pentecostal sect in Jamaica. My study of sects among Jamaicans in England supports this view; at least ten times as many people subscribe to Pentecostal doctrine as are members of sects.

In addition, census returns fail to give a true picture of Jamaican religious organisation. A proportion of those labelled 'Baptist' must belong to independent Baptist churches whose history was discussed in Chapter I; many of these are similar to Pentecostal sects. Furthermore, since 'Baptist' is a 'respectable' label, it would be reasonable to suspect that many people record themselves as Baptist for census purposes who are associated with, or even members of, quite other

---

[6] That this is the experience of other immigrant communities as well is borne out by a recent survey by Anthony Jackson: *The Irish in Britain*, London, Routledge and Kegan Paul, 1963. See especially Chapter VIII.

religious groups. There is, as I have shown, a long tradition of religious sectarianism in Jamaica; every year sees the rise of new religious leaders, some of them successful, some not. This suggests that Jamaicans are not very securely attached to their denominations, and prone to being influenced by new religious teachings. The remarkable rise of leaders like Bedward and Garvey bear this out. It is likely that many members of the Church of England and Baptist churches participate in sect worship as well, that the membership of the two dominant denominations and the membership of the sects overlap. This is suggested by the long association of the City Mission, the Salvation Army and the Baptists recorded in Chapter II: until the death of Raglan Phillips his followers could have described themselves as belonging to all three.

These arguments apply with most force to Jamaica, where there has been a long tradition of religious revivalism and where messianic leaders arise fairly often, but are less applicable to other British Caribbean islands. As was shown in Chapter III, the vast majority of sect members are Jamaican.[7]

The overwhelming Jamaican character of the sects may, perhaps, account for the higher proportion of small islanders than Jamaicans found in native English churches. Clergymen returning the questionnaire seldom mentioned Jamaica as the island their West Indian members came from. This tendency is well illustrated by one London Methodist congregation, the island derivation of whose members is set out in Table 14.

TABLE 14

*Island Derivation of the Members of
a Methodist Congregation*

Island	Number
St. Lucia	1
British Guiana	1
Dominica	1
Jamaica	2
Montserrat	4
Total	9

[7] No sect congregation is openly hostile to small-islanders. As has been shown, the congregation accepts as a member anyone willing to subscribe to its dogma and participate in its ritual. Perhaps the small-islander is in much the same position as the white man; he is welcome to participate, provided his participation does not appear to challenge the authority of the leader.

The following of another nonconformist church in London came entirely from Antigua and Montserrat.

Much is said about the failure of English churches to exert themselves in attracting migrants. Most of my informants agreed that they felt outsiders in English church services and that the English congregation did not really welcome their presence, but it is difficult to say how much this attitude is based on actual experience and how much it is an excuse for failing to go to church. As most West Indians feel that they should go to church, they feel obliged to invent excuses for not doing so.

Folk-myths provide a charter for the West Indians not going to church in England. One of these tells of the English clergyman's shaking hands with white people at the church door but not with West Indians, another of the clergyman's asking a West Indian who had attended a service not to come again. It is possible that such myths have a basis in actual happenings, but they are certainly garbled accounts of them. Almost any incident can be interpreted as revealing colour prejudice; one Pentecostal leader told me that a Church of England clergyman had asked him not to attend his services. Although the Pentecostal leader saw this as reflecting colour prejudice, a more reasonable interpretation is that the clergyman was exasperated with one who preached that all members of the Church of England are bound for hell and that Church of England clergymen are apostles of Anti-Christ.

In 1961 I talked with more than thirty London clergymen— Church of England, Congregationalist and Baptist—whose churches stood in areas of dense West Indian settlements. I found none of them prejudiced against West Indians though some felt that members of their congregations would not welcome them in large numbers.[8] Some of them had made efforts to attract West Indians; others explained that their normal work took up all of their time and that this would suffer if they were to direct their energies towards assimilating them into their congregations. As all or nearly all these churches stood in very poor residential areas in which a great volume of welfare work must be undertaken by the clergy, I see no reason to doubt the sincerity of this explanation.

Only where the clergyman has been specially interested in assimila-

---

[8] In churches that use a common Communion cup white members may object to taking the sacrament from it after West Indians have done so. This is not an important issue, and those clergymen who mentioned it to me had easily overcome white members' objections.

ting West Indians and has devoted a great deal of his time to doing
so is there a large West Indian following. This requires not only a
special interest in West Indians, a sympathy for their problems, an
infinite fund of tact, patience and enthusiasm, but also a great deal of
specialist knowledge that the average clergyman cannot reasonably
be expected to have. Lack of knowledge about the West Indies is
liable to be interpreted as lack of interest and sympathy; the distinc-
tions between Jamaicans, Barbadians and Trinidadians may not
appear important to the Englishman—but they are very important
to the West Indian.

At least three clergymen in the London area have had conspicuous
success in attracting West Indians to their churches. The Reverend
T. S. Burghart, until recently Congregationalist minister at Queen's
Park, had about a hundred attend a special service of thanksgiving
for the Caribbean Federation and about five times as many for another
special service at which a Congregationalist clergyman from the
West Indies gave the sermon. The Reverend D. Mason of the Lan-
caster Road Methodist church, North Kensington, who is specially
interested in the problem West Indian migration poses for the
churches, had an average West Indian attendance of about twenty
out of a total congregation of about sixty in 1961. On special occasions
about ninety people attended services, of whom between thirty and
forty were West Indians. He thought of the West Indian following of
his church as about forty, though not all of these attended every
service.[9]

In Tottenham, a relatively new area of dense West Indian settlement, the Reverend Clifford Hill had in 1963 an average West Indian
attendance of between forty and fifty at his Baptist church. For
special services, such as one to celebrate Jamaica's independence, he
has had more than a thousand. His West Indian following has increased considerably over the last two years.

I have mentioned these three congregations individually to show
the degree of success that a clergyman of one of the major denominations can have if he makes special efforts to attract West Indians. A
few other London clergymen have been similarly successful, but
most see little of West Indians except when their services are required at marriages, baptisms and funerals.

Nearly all clergymen I talked with were against encouraging West
Indians to hold their own services separately; they felt they could not

[9] Personal communication, 26 January 1961.

condone religious *apartheid*. This feeling was so strong that some have tried to incorporate independent Pentecostal groups into their congregations when approached by a Pentecostal leader seeking somewhere for his group to meet. Such experiments have never been successful and the Pentecostal group has usually ended up using the church hall when this was available. As I showed in Chapter III, finding a suitable room or hall for the group to meet in is a very important factor in the success of a new West Indian Pentecostal congregation.

Although few clergymen of established churches in England make any great effort to persuade West Indians to join their congregations, most of them maintain excellent relations with the independent West Indian sect congregations in their neighbourhoods. Indeed many of these sect congregations could not function without the goodwill of clergymen of the established churches. To hold a baptism service a sect must be able to borrow a church with a tank suitable for baptism by total immersion; baptism is a very important rite to all Pentecostal sects. English clergymen are also often asked to perform marriage ceremonies for sect members.

The Unitarians, despite the gulf in ritual and belief separating them from Pentecostal sects, always seem particularly well disposed towards them and remarkably tolerant of what to most English Christians must appear startlingly bizarre religious practices. In one district a Pentecostal group in the process of breaking away from one of the larger West Indian sects was looking for somewhere to meet and arrived at a Unitarian service one Sunday. It is possible that the leader, unacquainted with Unitarians in the West Indies, took them for a kind of Pentecostal sect. After the service, at which the West Indians amazed the Unitarian congregation with loud ejaculations of 'Hallelujah', he discussed his difficulties with the Unitarian clergyman. As it was agreed that their two forms of worship were incompatible in the same service it was agreed that the Pentecostal leader should borrow the church hall when the Unitarians were not using it. Other Pentecostal groups have also made use of these premises from time to time.

Another Unitarian hall in London was for two years used by a Pentecostal sect, until the sect membership had shrunk so much that it could conveniently meet in the sitting-room of a member's house. The Unitarian minister used to attend some of its services and was prepared to accept its manner of worship as a valid form of Christianity, even if very different from his own.

2. *The Seventh Day Adventists*

The Seventh Day Adventists, a wealthy, well-organised, central-ised group, have been operating in England since long before the great post-war increase in West Indian migration. They differ from most other religious groups in England in that they keep the sabbath on Saturday and taboo the use of tea and coffee by members. In some respects they are like the Pentecostal sects; they emphasise millennial doctrines and expect a high degree of congregational participation in their services.

Questionnaires returned by Seventh Day Adventist clergy re-vealed a remarkably large West Indian following (see Table 15):

TABLE 15

The Participation of West Indians in Seventh Day
Adventist Congregations

Town	Number of West Indian Members	Percentage of West Indian Members
Bedford	150	60
Birmingham	150	60
Coventry	7	11
Derby	18	33
Gloucester	10	20
Huddersfield	30	75
Ipswich	9	11
Leeds	14	18
Liverpool	3	6

In London, nearly all offices are held by West Indians in the Brixton congregation; two or three in the Chiswick one.

The Adventists differ from most denominations in England in that they proselytise vigorously and systematically. In January and February 1961 the Chiswick congregation distributed 20,000 hand-bills to houses in Acton. These were followed up by personal calls by the 30 per cent of the Chiswick congregation who were actively engaged in proselytisation. It is likely, as so many West Indians take part in campaigns of this kind, that the Adventists are particularly successful in recruiting from among the lonely migrants without friends, relatives or other social contacts in England.

The migrant can find satisfaction in Adventist churches that he

TABLE 16

West Indian Office Holders in the English Congregations Investigated

Town	Youth Leader	Deacon	Mission Leader	Sabbath School Teacher	Church Board	Total
Derby	1	1	0	1	1	4
Gloucester	0	1	0	0	0	1
Huddersfield	1	3	0	1	2	7
Ipswich	1	1	1	0	0	3
Leeds	1	2	0	1	0	4
Liverpool	0	0	0	0	0	0
Luton	0	2	0	0	0	2
Oxford	0	0	0	0	0	0
Reading	0	0	0	0	0	0
Southampton	0	0	0	0	0	0
Totals	4	10	1	3	3	21

might not find in other churches. He is given work to do in his spare time and is made to feel that his contribution is worth while; he can feel that he is a member of a group with common aims and values.[10] Adventist congregations strive to make the stranger, whether white or coloured, feel at home, and the welcome they extend goes far beyond the conventional clerical handshake at the church door; this helps further to explain their remarkable success among West Indians.

Immigrants are made to feel that they are participating fully in the life of the Adventist congregation very soon after they have joined it. In other churches they might, perhaps, have to wait longer before they could feel they were making a contribution. Also, because of the Adventists' very efficient organisation, a member moving his place of residence does not lose contact; he is put in touch with, and often becomes a member of, another congregation on moving to another town. West Indian members of other churches are more often lost when they move.

[10] I cannot say to what extent the Seventh Day Adventists resemble Pentecostal churches in sociological characteristics; this would require a detailed study. However, I suspect that West Indians can 'withdraw' into Seventh Day Adventist congregations in much the same way as they can into Pentecostal ones. The Seventh Day Adventist church in England is in a stage of development which the West Indian sects will not reach for some time. It is thus most like the English Pentecostal sects.

3. *The Migrants and English Pentecostalism*

When I started this study in 1961 there were about eighty West Indian sect congregations in Britain. There were nearly one thousand native English Pentecostal congregations. Most of these belonged to the two big organisations, the Assemblies of God and the Elim Church[11] but there were several small native English organisations as well. In many respects the history of their development resembles that of the Churches of God discussed in Appendix II and it covers the same period. English and imported West Indian sects differ very little in belief and ritual. The main difference in ritual is that the latter 'wash the feet of saints' whereas the former do not.[12]

West Indian migrants do not join the English Pentecostal churches to any greater extent than they do non-Pentecostal ones. No English congregation is all West Indian and few have even a large West Indian membership. Indeed they appear to be less popular among West Indians than the Seventh Day Adventists are. This may be partly because the migrant, familiar with the American-Caribbean Church of God type of Pentecostal worship, finds the English manner of running a service strange, and in any case, as we have seen, religious self-help comes naturally to him.

Most English Pentecostal congregations are small, very tightly knit groups. Very often members are linked by ties of kinship and inter-marriage. It is hardly to be expected that groups of this kind would be very welcoming to coloured strangers, especially when these prove to be innovators.

Many rank-and-file English Pentecostals, as well as some of the leaders, are indignant at the importation of new, rival Pentecostal sects from Jamaica. West Indians tend to be suspected of heresy, and if this does not lead to open hostility, it often prompts the English Pentecostal to attempt to correct the beliefs of the newcomer, to try to bring him back to the fold. The West Indian may bitterly resent this as patronage. Talking with tongues, the rite common to all Pentecostal churches, can be an important issue here. The English Elim Church holds that no more than three people should talk with tongues at the same service. To most West Indian Pentecostals this is an intolerable restriction and may even be regarded as a white

---

[11] These are distinct from the American Assemblies of God and Elim Foursquare Gospel churches. But their historical links with these have been far closer than with the southern branch of American Pentecostalism represented by the Church of God. The history of British Pentacostalism is outlined in Appendix III.

[12] This rite is described in Chapter VII.

man's conspiracy to prevent the black man from approaching God.

It is not unusual for religious groups very close to one another in ritual and belief to be less tolerant of one another than they are of groups more distant from them. This applies to relations between West Indian and native English Pentecostal sects. Generally the more orthodox English churches are more tolerant of West Indian sects than English Pentecostal sects are.

West Indians who have been here for a long time have flirted with English Pentecostal churches during their early days in England because there were then hardly any West Indian sects for them to join. Some remained members of English sects, but most of them quarrelled with the leaders and launched out on their own. British Pentecostal leaders have complained to me that until the large influx of West Indians they had little trouble in maintaining discipline in their congregations. A member who was 'disfellowshipped' could find no other Pentecostal group willing to accept him, but now, to quote one leader, 'he has only to walk round the corner'. This is even more of a problem for the West Indian sects.[13]

Perhaps as important as suspicion, doctrinal disagreement, and sectarian rivalry in the failure of West Indians to join British Pentecostal sects is the difficulty of finding them. This applies less to the Elim Church, whose meeting-places are generally well advertised, conspicuous buildings, than to other groups. I recall spending two days in Southampton locating its small Pentecostal assemblies; it is not surprising that none of them were found to have any West Indian members. Many groups do not have their own church but meet, as the West Indian sects do, in rented halls and rooms or in the homes of members; it can be very difficult indeed to find them, especially for a new arrival in England who does not know his way round and has no idea whom he should ask. The advantage Elim has in this is perhaps counterbalanced by its strict orthodoxy and strong central organisation, which many migrants find repellent.

With some outstanding exceptions Pentecostal sects in England are little addicted to open-air meetings in public places, whereas various West Indian sects hold them frequently in districts densely populated by their countrymen. One such group has used a van, equipped for the purpose with a loudspeaker, in the neighbourhood of Brixton market for about two years, and some of its members periodically undertake proselytising expeditions to other towns in a

[13] See Chapter V, section 2.

furniture van equipped as a caravan. Often more than half of the
religious groups proselytising at Hyde Park on a Sunday afternoon
are West Indian Pentecostal ones, whereas the native English sects
are seldom represented at all. A handful of English Pentecostal congregations do attract large West Indian followings. I have shown that
where this happens among non-Pentecostal churches it is because of
special qualities in the clergyman; this is equally true of Pentecostal
churches. The outstanding example is the Assemblies of God Congregation in Harrow Road, Paddington, whose pastor, the Reverend
Bernard Porter, has a particular sympathy for the problems of coloured people and a most acute, unsentimental understanding of their
difficulties. Two other Assemblies of God congregations, in the
Midlands, likewise have large West Indian followings.

4. *English Participation in West Indian Sects*

Many congregations have one or two English members. This
appears to be more common in the Church of God group, but occurs
in Jesus Name sects as well. One of the sects under discussion, the
Church of God of Prophecy, has an Englishman as its General Overseer in England, though all others are led by West Indians. East
London congregations of the New Testament Church of God had an
English following before 1958, and one leader claimed that his was
considerable, but no sect service I have attended has had more than
three or four white people present. Usually there are none at all.
(This is excepting the parties of missionaries from foreign lands who
sometimes attend large conventions and rallies, and white children
attending Sect Sunday Schools.)

Sometimes I recorded the presence of the same white Pentecostals
at the services of different sects during the one week; some of them
appear to wander from sect to sect without becoming attached to
any. But others remain with the same sect for months, or occasionally
years. The leader of the Church of the Living God for a time held
services in Reading together with a local English female Pentecostal
leader, but they soon fell out and have not co-operated since.

The English Pentecostals involved in West Indian sects are anything but a homogeneous group. Some of them are young, in their
twenties, and others are over sixty. Some are married and some are
single. Though most are, of course, manual workers, a very few
come originally from the middle classes. All of them have been
associated with English Pentecostal groups, particularly the Elim
Church or the Assemblies of God, at some time in their lives and have

either left them because, as they say, 'these churches are dead' or have been thrown out for heresy, as has been suggested to me by two West Indian Congregation leaders.

Most of them (all but two of those I have known) have tried to establish themselves in positions of leadership within the congregation. One man came close to success in the City Mission. On one occasion he was commissioned by the bishops or claimed to have been commissioned by them to watch over the London congregation while they were in the West Indies. Despite this his influence in the congregation was less than that of the three West Indian leaders. He became discouraged and finally left.

Although members always make such people welcome at services and permit them to preach, pray and testify as 'the Spirit leads', they are nevertheless kept at a certain distance, and any attempt to interfere in the running of the congregation is resented. Some of them are aware of this and have complained to me about it. All I have talked to are critical of what appears to them to be the West Indians' haphazard way of running their congregations and their unpunctuality in arriving at services, and feel that they could run things better.

Because of the willingness of West Indians to accept them so far but no farther, English 'saints' are seldom satisfied members and frequently become involved in disputes. West Indians are particularly likely to resent the arrogance with which many of them claim greater competence than West Indians in interpreting scripture; it is felt that they are claiming special privilege because they are white.

Very few of these people remain members of a sect congregation for long, although while they are they participate intensively, attending nearly all services just as nuclear members do. Except for one married couple, who belonged to a Jesus Name sect for four years,[14] none have stayed for more than eighteen months, and most much shorter times.

When they leave the congregation they do so without trying to take a following with them; their going never causes a split; nor do they appear to transfer their allegiance to another sect congregation as West Indians do. A married couple who attended City Mission meetings during 1961 is not now, as far as I have been able to discover, attending the services of any other West Indian sect,[15] nor is

---

[14] Recently (early 1964) this couple led a breakaway faction in a South London Jesus Name sect. It is too early yet to know how successful they have been.

[15] Recently (1964), after a lapse of two years, I found them attending a Jesus Name sect in North London.

the man with the 'gospel van', who is suspected by some City Mission members of having returned to 'the world'.

The presence of Europeans in some sect congregations is thus not an important factor in congregation fission, though it is possible that they are sometimes the source of heresies that cause dissension after they have left. But I have no firm evidence of this.

XI

SATISFACTIONS FOR THE INDIVIDUAL

WHY do West Indians join sect congregations? This question cannot be answered entirely in terms of the migrants' place in English society; the development of sect congregations as described in preceding chapters is not merely a reaction to the problems of settling down in an unfamiliar social environment, though as I shall show later, this is one of the factors involved.

1. *In the West Indies*

The reasons for sect membership in the West Indies have already been explained.[1] Under slavery the only forms of voluntary organisation permitted were religious. Although a political reaction to the slave's helplessness was sometimes sought in rebellion, slave uprisings were short-lived and never successful. As a result, the slave was forced to seek a magico-religious solution to his problems. These were not only problems directly associated with his status as a slave but also those of any uprooted population whose social organisation has been largely broken and whose cultural values are threatened. The magico-religious reaction was an attempt to solve the problem of insecurity generally. Political deprivation and slave status were only aspects of this.

The situation did not change in essential respects with the abolition of slavery, and by this time the slave population had been thoroughly exposed to Baptist Christianity. This reinforced the already crystallised pattern of religious leadership, and, if it were not already present, gave it a messianic twist. The dichotomy between the wicked world, in which sin and injustice were rampant, and the Kingdom of God, characterised by justice and love, was tailor-made for people undergoing rapid social change, uncertain of their values, and aware that all avenues to power, influence and status in the society at large were closed to them.

The Negro had little or no chance of achieving high status. As a political leader of the under-privileged he risked the wrath of those who held political power, and would be crushed before he had marshalled an effective following. But he could become a religious

[1] See Chapter II, section 2.

leader, and because this was the only possible avenue of leadership it became a pattern. The last years of slavery and its aftermath saw the blossoming of Negro Christianity and the rise of a multitude of religious leaders.

Some of these leaders acquired political or social reformist aims as well as religious ones. The tradition of religious-political action has always been strong in Jamaica, extending through Deacon Bogle of the Morant Bay rebellion, Bedward and Garvey, to the Ras Tafarians of the present day. These movements have sought to alter society; their model was inspired by the values of the New Testament, especially the equality of all before God. In a sense, they sought to establish the Kingdom of God on earth.

Other leaders saw the world as irredeemably wicked and the lot of the dispossessed as hopeless. They did not try to alter it, but turned their backs on it, seeking a purely magico-religious solution to the economic and social problems besetting their followers.

The two traditions exist side by side and are not distinct. Ras Tafarianism, for example, both ignores the world and wishes to alter it. Pentecostal sects in their Jamaican form represent the left wing of the second tradition, though as I have shown, even these must come to terms with the world on certain issues. Both types of religious movement draw their following from among those who find their aspirations frustrated and their condition hopeless, by offering magico-religious panaceas for the ills of the very poor who can never hope to be otherwise. Dire poverty is a condition of existence for a large part of the populations of West Indian islands, especially Jamaica; there is nothing fanciful about the situation which religion in its various forms seeks to ameliorate.

Pentecostal sects (like many others) offer members a new set of values and a new self-respect. The meaningless drudgery of a life devoted to finding enough to eat becomes less in the service of God, or takes on a new significance as an apprenticeship for the hereafter. Members who lack characteristics (occupation, education, possessions) carrying prestige in society at large, are persuaded that such things are unimportant; were not Christ and his disciples equally lacking in the things of the world? The 'world' has not treated sect recruits with conspicuous generosity, and in its terms they are lacking in status, poor and powerless, but these characteristics are precisely those which are pleasing to God. In their devotion to him, members make a virtue out of necessity, rejecting the values of the world which anyway they could not hope to achieve.

In rejecting the world, members claim to be superior to it. The values of the world are hateful to God, whereas Christian ones please him, so members have God on their side. They are specially chosen for immortality, whereas the world is condemned to destruction. Success in this world is almost synonymous with pride and devotion to the Devil; lack of worldly success is the badge of the saint— 'blessed are the meek'—'blessed are they that mourn'.

This is the ideology of withdrawal, of turning from the world to God. The individual confronted by grinding poverty must derive a certain satisfaction from being able to feel that he is superior to it. In addition, he finds consolation in his identification with the group, which may compensate for the instability of family organisation, in its turn a product of poverty and slavery. In England Pentecostals often say in their testimonies, 'When my father forsake me, my mother forsake me, Jesus keep me.' Perhaps this is more than a styl- ised ritual statement, and expresses the social isolation of the in- dividual in an anomic society.

In Jamaica, then, the individual is fleeing from the world into a sect congregation, is fleeing from poverty and the sense of frustration and personal inadequacy accompanying it. The society in which he lives sets him goals which he cannot attain. Rather than live with this frustration, with a crushing sense of personal inadequacy, he side- steps it and rejects the goals.

Perhaps in this frustration can be discerned the feeling of guilt and original sin that is a doctrinal cornerstone of all Pentecostal sects. The convert has in fact failed his God, even if through no fault of his own, and is in need of divine forgiveness. But the 'Blood of the Lamb' washes away all past shortcomings and allows him to start life again with a clean slate. Being 'born again' is more than a meaningless, conventional expression; the saint *is* born again into a new society with a new set of values. Freed from his burden of inadequacy he does indeed become a 'new man'. In discussing their conversion ex- periences Pentecostals often describe their feelings of relief and elation at laying aside their burden of sin. Social inadequacy becomes un- important, is cancelled out by joining a new, transcendent social group.

The same economic and social factors that oppress ordinary con- verts and lead to their deciding for Jesus and his church are opera- tive in the Pentecostal leader's choosing or being forced into his role. It is significant that all leaders come from the same social class as their members. Although their ability and drive may be considerable, their

attempts to reach positions of authority and leadership are frustrated
by poor education and low status. The only avenue to leadership that
does not depend on a fair degree of formal education is religion.
West Indian Pentecostal leaders may even glory in their lack of
education, as it might, they feel, come between the worshipper and
his God. By the confident inversion of conventional values so characteristic of Pentecostal sects, a disadvantage in the society at large
becomes an advantage in the sub-society of the saints.

Pentecostal leaders, however, seldom lack intelligence, and many
of them have considerable oratorical ability even though this may be
concealed by the observance of Pentecostal conventions of preaching.
These abilities can only be exercised within a religious group most of
whose rituals consist of talking, thus providing an ideal outlet for
eloquence. The religious leader, particularly if he is also an eloquent
preacher, is respected among West Indian Christians. People speak
with admiration, almost with awe, of his ability to sway congregations. In addition, according to sect ideology, he is the mouthpiece
of God.

Given the educational disadvantages of poorer people and the
example of religious leadership so common in West Indian society, it
is not surprising that so many people seek to express themselves and
outshine their fellows in this way. Nor is it the person of outstanding
ability alone who is able to achieve this sort of recognition and be
acclaimed by the group. Even one of very mediocre talents can be
sure of a hearing and be acclaimed with shouts of 'Praise the Lord!'

2. *In England*

The circumstances that have stimulated the growth of Pentecostal
sects in the West Indies and led people to join them have less force in
England. Modern England is not beset by poverty, people are not
forced to seek a magico-religious solution to otherwise insoluble
economic problems. Native English Pentecostal sects remain as a
memorial to such conditions in the past, but there have been no
revivals for more than a generation. Some are adapting very successfully to contemporary conditions and becoming more like Free
Church denominations; others continue to supply the needs of the
tiny minority unable or unwilling to cope with the changed but still
pressing demands of modern society.

West Indians are economically better off in England than they
were at home, even if less prosperous than they expected to be.
Despite higher living costs, unemployment and their holding the

poorer-paid jobs in public utilities and industry, migration has led to a less precarious existence. Some have been remarkably successful, able to buy houses and motor cars that they could never have afforded in the West Indies. Even the less lucky ones are at least preserved by National Assistance and Unemployment Benefits from the starvation that may well have been their lot at home. The volume of money remittances home testifies to the modest prosperity of the migrant population.

The existence of these sects in England cannot then be attributed to economic deprivation. Nor are sect members conspicuous for their lack of prosperity in England. The City Mission, at any time, has members who are relatively prosperous and members who are un-employed,[2] with, if anything, more relatively prosperous members holding permanent jobs than in the West Indian community gener-ally. Therefore an explanation for sect activity must be sought in the general difficulties experienced by the migrants in settling down, rather than in poverty.[3]

The migrant arriving in England finds himself confronted by differences in culture to which he must adjust himself. He comes as an isolated individual, perhaps knowing nobody in England, and he is lonely; he finds that skills he has learned in the West Indies are accepted reluctantly, if at all, by the English employers and trade unions. He finds English people tend to be reserved towards strang-ers. Sooner or later he is likely to experience colour prejudice or discrimination in some form.

Probably the most outstanding differences in culture confronting the migrant are those between an urban industrialised society and the agricultural one he has been used to. He must adjust to living and working in a big city, an isolated individual with neither family nor friends of long standing. Also the factory work at which he is em-ployed is likely to be very different from the work he has done at home, and unless the factory is a large one employing many other West Indians he is unlikely to establish close relationships with his workmates. The English climate precludes the kind of outdoor social life he has been used to in the West Indies, and much of his life must

---

[2] Only two members were unemployed for a long period during the winter of 1962–3. These were building workers prevented from working by the heavy falls of snow. Other members have been unemployed for short periods.

[3] There are middle-class non-Pentecostal sects in whose development poverty is certainly not a factor. Christian Science is one example. A less well-known one is the Christian Community, the followers of the German religious leader, Rudolf Steiner.

be spent huddled over a gas fire in a dingy but costly room in one of the drabber suburbs.

Seldom does he find England in reality the Land of Promise he has been led to expect. Jobs are difficult to get and well paid ones especially difficult. Often the only ones available are those which Englishmen are unwilling to take because they are ill paid, because they are dirty, or because they involve working inconvenient shifts. Although wages are high by Jamaican standards, so is the cost of living. The migrant saving money to return home or remitting it to dependants cannot afford a very high standard of living. As a result he is likely to be less well nourished than English workers are, and more prone to be away from work sick.

Sometimes English employers refuse to recognise the migrant's trade qualifications, if he has any, in the belief that West Indian trade standards are lower than English ones; so he may find himself forced to take a less skilled job than he held in the West Indies. Or perhaps the trade he has learned is not one in which there are many openings in England; he may have trained as a cooper and find that since wooden casks are little used in England there is no employment for him.

Over and above these difficulties and impinging on most of them is the problem of race relations. The migrant is marked off from the English population by more than cultural differences, such as the dialect of English he speaks and Caribbean food habits. His dark skin makes him conspicuous, and to most Englishmen it is the outstanding mark of his group membership. The differentiation of social groups in terms of skin pigmentation is nothing new to the West Indian, but to the Jamaican, at least, the Englishman's all-or-nothing application of the skin-colour criterion is something new. As nearly all people in Jamaica are of part African ancestry, degrees of pigmentation are recognised and are roughly correlated with position in the social class hierarchy. In England, on the other hand, there are only two categories: 'coloured' and 'non-coloured'; and coloured people are all treated as outsiders. The West Indian of light skin pigmentation is puzzled at not being accepted as 'more white' than his darker countrymen.

I think before discussing racial prejudice it is necessary to see it against a general background of inter-group relations that have nothing to do with race. Initially many if not most Englishmen are mildly prejudiced against Africans, Asians and West Indians; but they are also to some extent prejudiced against Germans, Frenchmen,

Italians, Americans or Jews. A racial minority, however, is more conspicuous; its members differ physically from the general run of the population, so that members carry the badge of their group membership about with them. Because they are conspicuous they can more easily become the object of prejudice, discrimination and hostility. Perhaps a conspicuous minority attracts hostility simply by virtue of its being conspicuous. But it is worth remembering that minority groups can be conspicuous in other ways as well; their manner of life makes the gypsies conspicuous, a dialect of English the Irish, aggressive religious proselytisation the Jehovah's Witnesses, manner of dress the Mods and Rockers. All these minorities and many others besides attract a certain amount of prejudice, partly at least because members are conspicuous. Skin colour is not necessarily a more conspicuous badge of group membership than manner of life, dialect, religious behaviour or dress, but it is permanent and ineradicable; and so it is difficult for a member of a racial minority to be assimilated into the society at large.

The West Indian migrant finds that many Englishmen are prejudiced against West Indians and that some of them express this prejudice in discrimination. This takes various forms and ranges in intensity from a failure to say 'thank you' to the refusal of a job. The two areas of discrimination most important to the migrant, however, are undoubtedly housing and employment. Prejudice in these areas means that he competes in English society at a disadvantage; life is made just that much harder for him.

Whatever the diverse factors at work, it seems to the West Indians that prejudice causes English people to eschew social contact with them, putting pressure on them to live where other migrants live, thus further reducing their social contacts with the native population, making them even more conspicuous and helping to maintain prejudice against them. On the other hand, of course, because they can avoid unpleasant contacts with prejudiced people and find it more congenial to live among people of the same cultural background, many migrants choose to live in areas with dense migrant populations.

In employment too, discrimination is a major handicap to the migrant. Both employers and employees are likely to oppose the employment of West Indians, the former sometimes because they consider them unsatisfactory workers but more often because they shrink from offending their native English workers.

As in most instances of discrimination against minority groups, it is those who must compete with members of the minority who show most prejudice and favour discrimination. An overwhelming majority of the migrants are unskilled or semi-skilled workers who compete for jobs with their English opposite numbers. English workers who, since the war, have been in a strong bargaining position because of the shortage of labour, fear that the employment of West Indians will lead to a reduction in their wages and living standards, and perhaps to unemployment. This point of view gains support from the West Indians' lack of interest in trade unions and their activities.

Some employers maintain a quota, limiting West Indians to a fixed proportion of their labour force. This is defended by employers and employees on the grounds that if a larger proportion of West Indians were employed, the industry would get the reputation of being a coloured man's preserve and native English workers would leave. The status of an industry or occupation appears to be related to the number of West Indians it employs. Employers may be fearful that by employing West Indians they may so lower the status of the occupation as to inhibit the recruitment of English workers. Qualified West Indians applying for advertised vacancies may be refused employment because of such a quota system, and some employers refuse to engage any West Indians at all.

Many industries operate a policy of 'last in, first out' when reducing their labour force, a policy usually accepted as fair by trade unions. But because West Indians are often recent arrivals, it means that more of them are dismissed than white workers. This is likely to be interpreted by them as gross racial discrimination. West Indians are often employed in casual or unskilled work, particularly in the building trades. When the job ends they are out of work and must go through all the frustration of finding another one. They are also subject to being temporarily laid off if the weather is bad.

Because the West Indian has experienced discrimination so often he is likely to interpret all setbacks in terms of it. Any landlord who refuses to let accommodation to him is likely to be accused of discrimination whether this is the case or not, and any employer who tells him that an advertised vacancy is already filled is suspected of lying. Discrimination may well come to be a neurotic excuse for personal inadequacy and lack of success, a defence, a consolation in adversity and an excuse for any and all shortcomings. Perhaps not many migrants seek escape in neurosis, but discrimination is sufficiently common for the migrant to feel uncertain in his relationships with the white community, to feel that he is rejected. Finding the road to assimilation fraught with rebuffs, he gives up trying to associate with white people and comes to depend increasingly on the social resources of his own community. Prominent among these are the Pentecostal sects.

I think, nevertheless, it would be wrong to place too much emphasis on discrimination against coloured people as a factor in the development of sect activity in England. Racial prejudice is only one, albeit a very important one, of the difficulties faced by the migrant population in adapting to life in an unfamiliar type of society. I suspect that had there been no colour discrimination, sects would have been imported just the same. It is, I think, a mistake to see discrimination as the root cause of every mildly aberrant form of social behaviour in the West Indian community.

This is borne out by the near absence of racial exclusiveness in the sects themselves. We have seen that perhaps some sects are more racially exclusive than others, but even here it is not a marked tendency and may depend very much on the outlook of the congregation leader. When I began this study I expected difficulty in making contact with sect members, and I was surprised at the readiness with which a white man could be accepted by them, provided he does not endeavour to usurp the role of leader.[4] All leaders, and many rank-and-file members as well, are conscious that their congregation should not appear racially exclusive. Every one of the handbills advertising large meetings, conventions and rallies I have filed during the two years of this study, states specifically that 'all nationalities are welcome', and some leaders boast of the number of white people attending their services.

This derives partly from a genuine belief that the gospel is for everybody, God making no discrimination of race or colour. But it is partly also a matter of prestige. Leaders and members alike are conscious that the sects are group of low status, and a white following is felt to raise it in the eyes of the white community as well as in the eyes of other sects. Despite their ideology of world renunciation they are sensitive to what the world thinks of them and anxious to create a good public image. Leaders are eager to maintain good relations with society, provided always that this does not require too great a compromise on their part. Here also the conflict is apparent between the sect's orientation towards the ritual needs of members and the necessity of maintaining itself in and recruiting from a larger social group.

[4] See Chapter X.

Sect members are willing to tolerate or welcome individual white people in their services. Nor does group ritual ever explicitly express hostility to the white community generally. It is possible that in small congregations in which I was well known, members desisted from public expression of hostility out of deference to my feelings, but I doubt whether this was so. At large services, where I was sometimes the only non-West Indian in a congregation of five or six hundred, and unknown to most of those present, it is very unlikely that my being there would have inhibited expressions of hostility, if they had been a usual part of the service.

I would not go so far as to say there is *no* hostility to white society implicit in ritual expressions; some of them permit of this interpretation. When a member in his testimony contrasts the virtuous poverty of the Christian with the sinful wealth of the world, he is very probably thinking in terms of West Indians and English people. Private conversations with sect members support this view, though very few of them indeed would agree with one man, preoccupied with discrimination to the point of neurosis, who expressed doubt that there would be any white people at all in heaven.

Sect ritual expressions sometimes contain an element of satisfaction at poverty and rejection by society, and the Sermon on the Mount, among other texts, certainly provides a convenient doctrinal basis for this. Perhaps this explains its popularity. 'Blessed are the poor in spirit—blessed are they that mourn—blessed are the meek—blessed are ye when men shall revile you and persecute you, and shall say all manner of evil against you falsely, for my sake. . . . Ye are the salt of the earth' (Matthew v, 3–13). 'For my sake' can easily come to mean 'when your skin is black'.

A common theme in testimonies and preaching is the parable of Lazarus (Luke xvi, 9–31)—the beggar who was 'carried by the angels into Abraham's bosom' and the rich man who went to hell. Undoubtedly sect members derive a certain satisfaction from identifying with Lazarus and contemplating the future torment of those who in this life are more prosperous than they are and look down on them.

If the expressed religious object of West Indian sects be left on one side, then they are groups that exist for their own sake. They meet to celebrate their own social solidarity and their practical efforts are directed towards this end. Beside deriving satisfaction from group rituals, members derive satisfaction from group structure and organisation. Jamaican society tends to be anomic and amorphous; the society they find in England must appear to them even more anomic and amorphous. They do not understand English society; they are (except economically) largely outside its structure and are not called on to occupy satisfying social roles within it.

The Pentecostal sect provides opportunities for participation in group life. The roles it offers are derived from the New Testament, which for the uneducated West Indian guarantees their worthwhileness. Saints can act out the roles of evangelist, convert, religious teacher and sometimes even martyr as they are described in the Gospels, Acts and Epistles. The many offices within the congregation organisation provide other satisfying roles; as we have seen, most congregations have deacons, Sunday School teachers, youth leaders and so forth. Ritual withdrawal from the world is thoroughly consistent with this as few New Testament roles are appropriate to large-scale industrialised societies.

Part of the intense satisfaction felt by Pentecostal members is derived from role-acting and resembles the satisfaction that comes from playing an elaborate game. In addition the faithful filling of roles described in the New Testament is in itself felt to be pleasing to God; the roles themselves are ritual acts of worship. God is pleased when a saint slips into the role of 'bishop-exhorting-the-church', 'apostle-writing-an-epistle', 'peacemaker' and so forth.

Conflict, about which so much has been said in earlier chapters, provides excellent opportunities for performing biblical roles, and though it may lead to the extinction of a congregation now and then, it has the overall effect of stimulating West Indian Pentecostalism. The interest of the ordinary member is stimulated by the constant to-and-fro of sect building and fission; too much is happening for him to become bored with repetitive Pentecostal rituals. It is precisely when the congregation is running smoothly and meeting regularly that members are apt to become bored and start feeling that there is something amiss in the relationship of their church to God. Doctrinal disagreement stimulates the interest of a member in his roles, while fission may provide him with an opportunity of occupying new ones.

Very little sect activity takes place in the atmosphere of grim dedication conventionally associated with fundamentalist religious groups. For most of those involved, sects are fun. People attend services because they enjoy them. They enjoy dressing up in their best clothes; they enjoy being the centre of attention when they testify and preach; perhaps most of all they enjoy singing hymns and choruses, swaying their bodies and stamping in time to the music or dancing to it. Music is very prominent in sect activities; about half the time of an average service is devoted to singing. Sect meetings, especially well-attended ones, can be most exciting experiences, and there is no doubt that both members and those less firmly attached enjoy them thoroughly.

Members do not feel it inappropriate that they should enjoy religion and show that they are doing so; on the contrary, leaders often exhort their congregations to 'show that you are happy in the Lord'. Being happy is a positive religious value; not to feel elated during services indicates a defect in one's relationship to God. That happiness is to a degree mandatory does not appear to diminish members' spontaneous enjoyment.

3. *Sects and Assimilation*

As I have shown in the preceding chapters, West Indian like other Pentecostal sects think of society as divided into two: the saints—the saved, those devoted to God—and the 'world', those living in sin and devoted to the Devil. By performing group rituals they seek to approach closer to God and consequently to withdraw farther from the 'world'. Saints show little interest in the broader society of which they are members, except in so far as it is a reservoir of lost souls who might be persuaded to join them.

Ideally saints should be motivated by loyalty to God only; if their relatives are not saved they should cut themselves off from them. That they do not do so preserves a point of contact with the 'world'. But kin groups are almost the sole area of contact, and although they link saints to other West Indians, they link them only very tenuously to the rest of society.

Saints stand apart from other West Indians; they stand even farther apart from English people. As I have shown, they do not even have close contacts with English Pentecostal churches; they are not being assimilated to a religious minority already present in English society.

Quite definitely, as they are now, the sects are a stumbling-block to the assimilation of Britain's West Indian minority, providing as they do a magico-religious refuge from the stresses and strains of settling down in a new country. Saints are much farther from assimilation than non-Pentecostal West Indians because they erect cultural barriers to assimilation additional to those the migrant must encounter anyway.

Perhaps in Jamaica the saints' seeking religious consolation for hopeless poverty and social disorganisation is inevitable; their position is indeed hopeless. But in England the position of the West Indian minority is far from hopeless. Despite minor tensions and sporadic riots which tend to receive more publicity than their importance warrants, Britain does not have an acute race relations problem. The migrant may have difficulty in finding a job, but he does find one; some landlords are reluctant to rent him accommodation, but others are quite willing to do so. The migrant is not caught in a closed system. He can overcome the undoubted disadvantages of having a dark skin, and often does.

The thoroughgoing, obsessive, ritual withdrawal of the saint from the world appears to be out of all proportion to the actual difficulty of the situation he is withdrawing from. I think this can only be understood historically. As I have shown, there is in the West Indies a long tradition of seeking magico-religious rather than practical solutions to problems. This is particularly true of Jamaica, whence nearly all sect members have come.

Having said all this, I think that nevertheless sects have a positive role in the assimilatory process. During the earlier stages of assimilation they form a buffer between the immigrant group and society. They cushion the impact on the individual of a new way of life in a new type of society having unfamiliar values. They provide continuity between his old life in the West Indies and his new life in England. Perhaps, even if they initially impede assimilation, they facilitate it by greasing the wheels of social change in the long run. This is very probable because, as I have shown, the sects are changing rapidly. In this book I have described them at one stage in their development. Already some of them show signs of coming to terms with the 'world', of starting the slow process of development by which those of them that survive will one day become churches generally recognised as part of the English scene.

APPENDIX I

RESEARCH PROBLEMS AND TECHNIQUES

THE study of religious sects poses special problems for the anthropologist. Chief among these is that such sects provide no possible role for the outsider. One who attends their services is, almost by definition, either a member or one interested in becoming a member. It is the duty of the saints to take every possible opportunity of converting him. None of the sects I have discussed have any experience of anthropological research and since they see themselves in exclusively religious terms it is doubtful whether they would consider such research worth while.

Any non-West Indian who attempts to be a pure observer is the object of extreme suspicion; since the sect congregation sees itself as hostile to the world, a representative of the world can be up to no good. Many sect leaders are apprehensive that their running freelance churches contravenes English law and that churches that are not officially 'registered' are liable to be closed down by the 'authorities'. During the early phases of the enquiry, until I became well known, I was often suspected of being an agent of 'the Government' or of the Church of England, a kind of ecclesiastical dog-catcher.

Although there is no role for the outsider in a Pentecostal service he is invariably treated with extreme courtesy, largely in the hope that he will become a member, but partly also because the Bible ordains that all must be made welcome in God's house. But the restraint of all present is marked; the leader preaches more for the benefit of the stranger than for the benefit of the congregation. Ecstatic behaviour is likely to be restricted to the odd ejaculation of 'Hallelujah', lest the stranger's religious sensibilities be offended. Probably because of the dampening effect the presence of strangers, particularly non-West Indian ones, has on a West Indian Pentecostal service, they are usually introduced by the preacher, who by doing so vouches for their goodwill and acceptance of Pentecostal conventions.

I soon found, as I had found before, when working on a Pentecostal sect among Aborigines in Australia, that the only feasible approach was participation. To gain material of any but a very superficial kind it was necessary that my informants believed me to be a Pentecostal. Only then would they talk about their churches, confident that I would understand their problems and sympathise with them.

Participant observation was the only role open to me, but it created its own problems. I did not want to be restricted to participating in only one sect congregation; I wanted to move freely among them, and yet, as I have shown, Pentecostals are always members of one congregation or another at a particular time. I found that congregations competed for me, nor was it any use insisting that I was an independent kind of Pentecostal who did not want to be a member of a congregation. On the one occasion on which I was foolish enough to suggest this, I was told sternly that the Bible enjoined membership of a church on all God's saints and that if I did not belong to a church I was not of God. The only solution to this problem was to present myself as one who was still looking for the sect that satisfied all the requirements of the Gospels and that I expected that one day God would indicate to me which congregation I should join. Besides ensuring my freedom of movement this role was useful in another way. It almost invariably led an informant to expound the doctrine of his own sect and provided me with an excellent opportunity of questioning him about it.

In sect worship my participation was limited to singing, praying, ritual ejaculations and sometimes preaching. I did not talk with tongues as this would have involved me too deeply with the congregation in which I did so. Word would have got around that I had been blessed, that God had shown me that this congregation was the one most closely in touch with him; leaders of other congregations would have been jealous. Apart from this I was not altogether confident of my ability to simulate ecstasy convincingly. It seemed better not to try than to risk destroying *rapport* by failing to carry it off.

Preaching presented special problems, particularly early in the project when I often did not have a detailed knowledge of the doctrines of the sect concerned and so risked saying the wrong thing. Except with the sects I knew very well I restricted myself to reading a longish passage from the Bible and adding a few comments. The Book of Psalms was particularly useful for this, as from the Pentecostal point of view it is doctrinally neutral, and it was always possible to find a psalm suitable to the occasion. This manner of preaching was, of course, at variance with Pentecostal practice, but it was accepted that God had led me to participate in this way. The same difficulties arose when I was asked to pray aloud, but this happened very rarely.

Although I was accepted, up to a point, I was certainly always thought of as something of an oddity. There was no role into which I could be fitted precisely. Some thought of me as a clearing-house for information about other sects operating in England. Others sought advice on methods of raising money to buy buildings, or the prospects of evangelistic campaigns in other areas. Sometimes I was asked to write references to help members to get jobs or to advise on the education of their children. As I was often present at 'business meetings' called to settle questions of church policy, such as the way funds should be spent, I often found myself in the midst of factional disputes, with each side demanding my support. When asked to speak in such a meeting I tried always to present the alternatives without appearing to take sides. If, as was sometimes the case, I did not understand what the dispute was about, or if I felt that whatever I said would be misconstrued by one side or the other, I took refuge in the role of 'peacemaker' and called on God to heal the breach and reveal the correct course of action to his people. As I was particularly interested in the processes whereby new sects came into being I was anxious to avoid becoming a factor in it. Besides, if I were to get a rounded picture of what was happening it was essential that I remain on good terms with the leaders of both factions. I suspect that problems of this kind are not peculiar to the study of ecstatic religious groups but must be faced by anyone engaged in a study of conflict.

I doubt that my presence at a sect meeting had an appreciable effect on the heat of disputes or on their outcome. The issues involved were too important to the participants for them to care whether or not they were making a good impression on an outsider. On this I can only say that disputes I witnessed appear to have been neither more nor less rancorous than those that were described to me. Members were often apologetic about both the unseemliness of ruction in God's house and the frequency of fission among West Indian sects, but I do not think they were surprised at it or much embarrassed that I should witness it. As we have seen, it is part of their creed at one and the same time to express regret at the disunity of God's people and to welcome it as a sign that the Second Coming is imminent.

When I started work on this project I felt that my not being a West Indian, my being white and of superior education to all my informants would prove disadvantageous. I am now of the opinion that this was not so, that had I been more like my informants in background, I would have been forced to participate in ways not justified by my research interests.

Taking notes in a notebook was not possible during services. When I tried to do this early in the project I found that it made people suspicious. On one occasion I was asked to stop doing so. This was because it was felt to be inappropriate in a religious service to do things other than worship God, rather than because the saints were suspicious of what I was writing. Finally I worked out a compromise acceptable to members. Instead of using a notebook I used loose sheets of paper clipped inside the covers of a Bible. As most saints annotate their Bibles, often during services, no objection could be made to my appearing to do the same.

Rather to my surprise I found that no objection was raised to my tape-recording services. Indeed, some congregation leaders became so enthusiastic about it that at one time I had more requests to make recordings than I could handle. Although recordings provided a great deal of valuable material that could not be written down verbatim in the course of the service, there were disadvantages too. The machine required constant attention, as the volume of sound varied enormously. In a largish hall it was impossible to record verbal rituals delivered very far from the microphone because of loud interjections from those close to it. Very often the most interesting parts of a service were completely drowned by shouts of 'Hallelujah' and 'Praise the Lord'.

At the beginning of the project I had considered recording a sample of services, but I soon abandoned the idea and recorded only those that I knew in advance would provide material that would justify the expense of the tape and the time spent going through the tapes afterwards.

No sect congregations were averse to my taking photographs (with a flash-gun) during services. I photographed all types of service except funerals. Saints were avid for prints of themselves engaged in religious activities, and nearly all the invitations I received to regular services and conventions included a request that I should take photographs of it. My problem was only to curb this enthusiasm, as from my point of view a photographic record was of minor importance.

APPENDIX II

HISTORY OF THE CHURCH OF GOD

Most of the material in this appendix has been provided by C. W. Conn's Like a Mighty Army Moves the Church of God (*Cleveland, Church of God Publishing House,* 1955).

THE Church of God is an offshoot of a nineteenth-century 'Holiness' movement. In 1886, in the Unicoi mountains between Tennessee and North Carolina, an aged Baptist minister, Richard G. Spurling, called on a small congregation at the Barney Creek meeting-house to 'take the New Testament, or law of Christ, for your only true rule of faith and practice; giving each other equal rights and privilege to read and interpret for yourselves as your conscience may dictate, . . . and . . . sit together as the church of God to transact business as the same . . .' Spurling and eight followers formed the Christian Union. Shortly afterwards he died and leadership passed to his son, Richard Spurling Junior.

For ten years there was little increase in membership; the Christian Union was one tiny Holiness church among many others. Then in 1896 it joined with another such group led by a Methodist, William Martin, and two Baptists, Joe Tipton and Milton McNabb, in holding a revival campaign at Camp Creek, North Carolina. Although this appears to have been moderately successful, the meetings got a little out of hand. Conn says (op. cit.): 'Fanatic teachers came among the group and led many of them into a pathetic pursuit of a religious rainbow's end. According to their doctrine, there were many other "baptisms of fire" awaiting those who had received the baptism of the Holy Ghost. Christians were misdirected to seek the "holy dynamite", then the "holy lyddite" and finally the "holy oxidite". These equivocal chemical-religious terms were used to designate the alleged progressive steps of spiritual power.' Possibly these excesses, which also occurred in the early histories of other Pentecostal groups, were a reason for the anti-Holiness demonstrations that continued in this area until about 1902. During one of these the Christian Union's newly-built church was burned down.

The large following attracted by the revival had faded away by 1902 when some twenty of the faithful remnant founded the 'Holiness Church at Camp Creek'. Six new members joined in 1903, among them A. J. Tomlinson, an itinerant Bible-vendor from Indiana who immediately became influential in the movement, was ordained by Spurling, and acted as pastor of the local congregation while Spurling evangelised elsewhere. At the end of 1904 a local congregation in Cleveland, Bradley County,

Tennessee united with the Holiness Church and Tomlinson moved there to minister to it; the headquarters of the church have been there ever since. Two more congregations were added in Tennessee and one in Georgia during 1906 and in January of that year the first Assembly of the growing church was held at Camp Creek. At this meeting it was decided to hold assemblies each year, that the rite of 'washing the feet of Saints' should be celebrated by each congregation at least once a year in accordance with John xiii, 4–17, that the use of tobacco should be discouraged among members because 'we believe the use of it to be contrary to the teaching of the Scripture, and as Christ is our Example, we cannot believe that he would use it in any form or under any circumstances' and that Sunday Schools should be established in areas where there were no congregations '. . . thereby opening the way for more permanent work'.

By 1906 the new sect had taken on most of the characteristics that distinguish it today, except for the name 'Church of God' which it adopted in 1907. This name was apparently adopted on biblical authority—though there is a legend that Tomlinson received it in a direct revelation while praying on a mountain.

The congregation in Cleveland soon became the largest and most influential one, with about sixty members in 1906. The Church of God was a rural sect, and as the town's population grew through migration from rural areas the Church of God's congregation grew as well. At this stage at least there was a marked preponderance of female members.

A Church of God preacher writing in 1910 describes the conditions of dire poverty in the rural areas which must have been one of the mainsprings of the movement in its early days: 'Some of the members of this church could not come to the meeting for want of clothing. I am told that some of their people will suffer want this summer on account of the winter being so severe that they could not work. A number of them asked me to bring them some clothing, as I had taken some there before. I saw little boys of six or eight years old, barefooted wading through icicles, the ground frozen two or three inches deep and the higher mountains covered with snow' (Conn, op. cit., p. 79).

By 1910 the Church of God had 1,005 members in thirty-five congregations, and membership has continued to increase down to the present day. In the United States membership is still concentrated in rural areas and small towns. In 1954 66 per cent of members lived in rural areas or in towns with populations less than 5,000, and only 14 per cent in towns with populations more than 25,000. This contrasts sharply with the situation in England, where West Indian migrants live mostly in big cities and Church of God members are exclusively urban industrial workers.

From the beginning the sect was torn by schism. There was a split over the doctrine of talking in tongues as early as 1909 and in 1919 a further one over tithing, which led to the formation of the Original Church of God.

By far the most serious split occurred in 1923 when Tomlinson, who had been undisputed leader for nearly twenty years, was impeached before the Supreme Judges' Court of the Church of God for, among other things, failure to account for funds. This led to a legal battle over the ownership of property which was only in 1927 settled against Tomlinson and in favour of the Church of God. Some congregations in the United States, including most of those in Dakota and perhaps an even larger proportion in the West Indies, followed Tomlinson.

On 8 April 1929, the followers of Tomlinson adopted the name 'Tomlinson Church of God' and this was used until 6 March, 1953, when they took the name 'Church of God of Prophecy'. They have never accepted the claim of their erstwhile brethren to be the only 'true' Church of God and refer to them as the 'Elders' Church of God'. In the West Indies the parent group is called the 'New Testament Church of God' and this name is also used in England. The followers of Tomlinson are called the 'Bible Church of God' in the West Indies and the 'Church of God of Prophecy' in England. To avoid confusion I am taking in this book the names in use among West Indians in England: New Testament Church of God for the parent group, and Church of God of Prophecy for the followers of Tomlinson.

The change of name from Tomlinson Church of God to Church of God of Prophecy in 1953 was necessitated by a further split. When Tomlinson died both his sons aspired to be the new leader. Milton Tomlinson was selected by the General Assembly but Homer Tomlinson, who had been Overseer for New York State, claimed to have been directly appointed by God. In the split that followed this dynastic squabble the majority of members appear to have followed Milton Tomlinson, who was still leading the Church of God of Prophecy in 1960. In the West Indies both brothers had a following, but here also most members appear to have followed Milton. In England the Church of God of Prophecy is the second largest of the West Indian sects whereas only one congregation follows Homer, and even in this one, members are not quite decided whether they are followers of Homer or an independent sect. Diagram A1 summarises the main fissions and changes of name in the Church of God in the United States. More recent splits among West Indians in England are discussed in Chapter V.

Like most other sects and all Pentecostal ones, the Church of God thought of itself as a missionary organisation from the outset. Evangelisation, the 'saving of souls', was at least as important as providing facilities for regular worship by members. Initially evangelism was confined to Tennessee, Georgia and South Carolina, but as the church increased in membership and resources its evangelists roamed farther afield: missionary activity in foreign lands was felt to be a natural extension of evangelism at home. There was neither organisation nor funds to deal with foreign missions until 1911, but this developed slowly until in 1954 an income of $535,000 was earmarked for overseas mission work.

Diagram A1. Development of the Churches of God

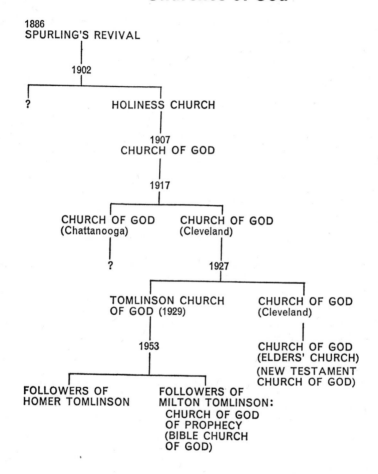

The Church of God has long been associated with the West Indies. Except for Canada, the Caribbean Islands were the first foreign territory to come under its influence. In 1909 Edmund Barr, a native of the Bahamas, attended a camp meeting in Florida and returned home to evangelise. In 1910 he was followed by an ex-Methodist minister, R. M. Evans and his family. This was the first Pentecostal incursion into the Bahamas and there were soon flourishing churches. At the same time some evangelism was undertaken in Cuba by Sam Perry, but no churches were established until many years later, in 1942.

About 1917 a Church of God missionary started work in the Argentine and two years later had two congregations and twenty-four members. By 1919 assistance was being sent to missionaries in Egypt and India as well.

A Barbadian church leader living in Jamaica led his flock into the Church of God in about 1917, but when it split in 1923 it seems that a far higher proportion of the Caribbean than the North American congregations followed Tomlinson; the foreign membership fell from 660 in 1924 to 360 in 1925. Conn admits that 'Tomlinson won a sizeable following in the Islands at the expense of the Church of God'. When, after being appointed first Overseer of Jamaica at the Assembly of 1924, E. E. Simons toured his province he 'was unable to find even one of the reported churches'. This does not mean that all the Jamaican congregations had gone over to Tomlinson, but rather that uncertainty about the leadership stimulated them to follow what was certainly already a well-established pattern; to split up into independent congregations recognising no outside authority. This tendency is marked among West Indian Pentecostal churches in England today.

By 1954 the Church of God (Elders' Church) had members in nearly all the islands of the Caribbean, in South America, Central America, Germany, India, China, Hawaii, Japan, Sicily, Spain, the Philippines, Nigeria, South Africa, Egypt, Palestine and Cyprus. The occurrence of the sect in so many areas outside the United States was not always due to the efforts of Church of God missionaries; often quite independent Pentecostal mission bodies, finding it difficult to finance their work, joined it with their flocks. A Pentecostal mission which had been operating independently in Tunisia since 1911 joined it in 1947 and a similar mission in Chile in 1954. By far the most important union of this kind was that of 1951 with the Full Gospel Church of South Africa, which had 57,000 members in 1954. In 1954 the overseas membership of the Church of God was approximately one-third of the total membership of 263,676 and it was thoroughly established as an international movement.

APPENDIX III

HISTORY OF THE ENGLISH PENTECOSTAL CHURCHES

Much of the historical material in this chapter is from Donald Gee's The Pentecostal Movement, *London, Elim Publishing Co. Ltd., 2nd ed. 1949.*

NATIVE English Pentecostalism stems from the late nineteenth-century revivals of Sankey and Moody, but did not crystallise as a separate movement until the early years of this century. Early British Pentecostals did not think of themselves as a separate sect; indeed they were against religious denominationalism. Some of them remained members of Church of England, Baptist, Congregationalist, Methodist or Presbyterian congregations all their lives.

The Great Welsh Revival of 1904 was followed by a similar quickening of religious enthusiasm in other parts of the British Isles; by the end of 1907 Pentecostal-type services accompanied by 'baptism of the Holy Ghost' were occurring at the Church of England parish church of All Saints in Sunderland. This was followed in 1908 by the formation of several Pentecostal groups in Scotland, Northern Ireland and Wales. In Wales a Congregationalist clergyman, Thomas Jeffreys, was among the important early leaders; Welsh influence in British Pentecostalism remains strong to the present day.

From its inception English Pentecostalism has been in close contact with similar movements abroad, particularly in Scandinavia and the United States. Early British and Scandinavian Pentecostals were inspired by reports of Pentecostal phenomena, possession by the Holy Spirit, in the United States, at Topeka in 1900, and at Galena in 1903, at Houston in 1904 and 1905, and at Los Angeles in 1906. The wide publicity given to the last led to visits by Scandinavian and British leaders to Los Angeles. But there appears to have been practically no contact with the other United States Pentecostal tradition, the Church of God, which was developing at the same time in Tennessee. As we have seen, in 1907 the Church of God established 'washing the feet of saints' as an obligatory ritual. This tended to cut them off from other North American Pentecostal traditions as well as from European ones.

Almost from the beginning Pentecostals on both sides of the Atlantic interested themselves in foreign missions, and by 1910 the English ones were supporting missionaries in India and China. As there was, at this time, no central Pentecostal organisation, a missionary enterprise was usually supported by one local congregation or by a small group of them, and missionary bodies existed more or less independently. It was not until 1925 that one of these, the Pentecostal Missionary Union, founded in 1905, was incorporated in the Assemblies of God. Some Pentecostal missionary bodies, such as the Slavic Gospel Association, still maintain an independent existence, and their missionaries home on leave tour Pentecostal congregations, preaching and raising funds. As they are not affiliated with any one Pentecostal church organisation they can usually count on support from several of them, even West Indian ones.

During its early history the Pentecostal movement was little concerned with orthodoxy. There was no well worked-out doctrine against which the beliefs and practices of local congregations could be measured. Some of them emphasised prophetic utterances of members and held these to embody divine directives on church government. This doctrine was being singled out as a heresy by other Pentecostal congregations by about 1916 and led to the formation of the Apostolic Church—the earliest major breakaway Pentecostal sect in England.

Partly because of the challenge of the Apostolic Church during the 1920's, the other English Pentecostal congregations felt the need for some form of church organisation; and this led ultimately to the formation of the Elim Church and the Assemblies of God, the two largest Pentecostal groups in England.

Elim developed out of the revival campaigns of George Jeffreys in Northern Ireland, the Elim Pentecostal Alliance being formed at Belfast in 1916. In 1921 it was established in England and Wales.

The Assemblies of God was formed in 1924 in reaction to the inroads of the Apostolic Church in Wales. The Welsh congregations flirted with the idea of joining the American Assemblies of God which had come into being in 1914 and this apparently forced the English congregations, rather against their will, to agree to some kind of union.

Throughout the history of Pentecostalism in England, church government and centralisation have been major issues. The early leaders did not see themselves as forming new denominations but rather as reacting against denominationalism; they thought of themselves as revitalising the Protestant churches rather than as competing with them. But since the established Protestant churches failed to be revitalised by revival, the campaigns left a residue of small Pentecostal congregations all over the country. These for a long time resisted being organised into denominations, and a few of them still remain fully independent.

This issue was raised once more in 1940 when George Jeffreys, who had founded the Elim Church, broke away from it to form the 'Bible Pattern Church Fellowship'. The Elim Church had become increasingly centralised and denominational and Jeffreys saw this as a frustration of his life's work. A doctrinal issue was involved in this split as well; Jeffreys came to support British Israel doctrines, the view that the British people are the lost tribes of Israel, or one of them; this was unacceptable to other leaders of the movement. About thirty congregations followed Jeffreys but some of these have since returned to the Elim fold. It remains to be seen whether the Bible Pattern Church Fellowship will long survive the death of Jeffreys in February 1963; at present Elim is rapidly eroding its membership.

The Apostolic Church which parted from the mainstream of Pentecostal development in 1916 split into the Apostolic Church and the United Apostolic Faith Church. The former, at least, has progressively modified its extreme doctrine of the relevance of prophecy to Church government and both are now members of the Pentecostal Federation.

Today, then, the following native-born Pentecostal churches are operating in England: the Elim Church, the Assemblies of God, the Full Gospel Testimony, the Bible Pattern Church and the United Apostolic Faith Church. Besides these there remain a few quite independent congregations, some of them of very long standing.

Table A1 lists the approximate number of congregations belonging to some of these sects in England and Wales.

TABLE A1

Number of Congregations belonging to British Pentecostal Sects

Sect	Number of Congregations
Elim	140
Assemblies of God	511
Bible Pattern	3 to 20
Apostolic Church	250 (in British Isles)
United Apostolic Faith Church	12
Total Number of Congregations	933

The figures for the Elim Church and Assemblies of God are taken from the official yearbooks of these sects. Bible Pattern does not issue a yearbook and leaders are reluctant to estimate how many congregations still follow them. The Apostolic Church figures are estimates by leading members in London, but members of the other sects doubt whether it has as big a following as it claims. The figures quoted are for the British Isles, including Scotland and Ireland, and it is likely that less than half of these congregations are in England and Wales.

Elim and the Assemblies of God are the largest Pentecostal groups in England, many times larger than even the largest of the West Indian sects. The strength of Elim is most apparent in its strong central organisation and emphasis on orthodoxy. The Assemblies of God is a very much looser kind of organisation; its constituent assemblies often do not even call themselves 'Assemblies of God', names like the 'Pentecostal Fellowship',

'Pentecostal Assembly', or 'Bethel Full Gospel Church' being common in the 1962–3 yearbook.

Diagram A2. The Development of English Pentecostal Sects

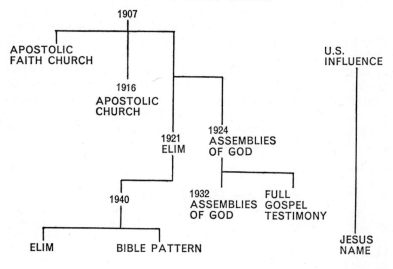

APPENDIX IV

HISTORY OF THE CITY MISSION

My historical information is derived from conversations with City Mission members in London and a handwritten copy of a printed account of the life of Raglan Phillips not available in England. This was supplied by Light Brigade Salome Morris whom I should like to thank specially for it. I am also indebted to Major Austin of the Salvation Army for an enlightening conversation on the history of this sect and the early days of the Salvation Army in Jamaica.

THE founder of the City Mission, W. Raglan Phillips, was born in Bristol in 1854, the son of a soapmaker. At the age of seventeen he went to Jamaica to work as an estate book-keeper. He was successively attorney's clerk, surveyor and printer and publisher of the *Westmoreland Telegraph* at Savanna-la-Mar. He also managed a 'brass and reed band', which doubtless stood him in good stead in the revival campaigns he undertook later.

After a period spent investigating spiritualism Phillips became a Baptist and applied for the ministry, but was rejected. This apparently led him to join the Salvation Army, and he asked General Booth in 1887 to send officers to Jamaica. The next year he commenced evangelisation with Booth's officers at Bluefields near Savanna-la-Mar in Westmoreland Parish. From 1889, when the Salvation Army officers were withdrawn, he continued the work alone, and apparently independently, under the name of 'Salvation Army of Jamaica'. In 1894 Booth asked him to come to London for a consultation on the work in Jamaica. Booth appointed him as staff officer and, in return, he brought his 123 officers and the 8,000 followers he claimed back into the Salvation Army.

In 1906 and 1907 he was lent by the Salvation Army to several Baptist churches as an evangelist and took part in a spectacular revival. Members of the City Mission say that faith-healing was conspicuous in this revival and, perhaps more significant, that the first cases of talking with tongues in Jamaica occurred.

After the revival, Phillips became a Baptist minister within the Jamaican Baptist Union, serving for seven years in Clarendon Parish and five years in St. Thomas Parish. In 1924 he was in charge of the Thompson Town Baptist church, where he instigated a second revival. This spread to Chapelton, Westmoreland Parish and Hanover Parish and, like the earlier one, is remembered for faith-healing. Two of the three bishops now leading the City Mission joined Phillips during these campaigns, and the third in Kingston the following year.

It appears that until this campaign and during his period as a Baptist

minister Phillips's following was not distinct from the Salvation Army one.
Most of the present leaders, including all those in England, have been
Salvation Army officers. But between 1925 and Phillips's death in June,
1930, the City Mission diverged more and more from the Salvation Army;
the name City Mission was being used as early as 1925. Nevertheless the
break does not appear to have been final at the time of his death as he was
buried by a Salvation Army officer, Brigadier C. Smith.

During Phillips's lifetime the City Mission became increasingly Pentecostal and progressively more like the Churches of God. Today the only
difference in ritual between them is that the City Mission does not 'wash
the feet of saints'. It does, however, retain two Salvation Army characteristics not shared by the Churches of God: the use of uniforms and a
system of rank.

APPENDIX V

TESTIMONY

1. BRETHREN, this is another privilege again. As I listen to that song, some-one has said that I am a child of a King. We do not know what we may be like, but one thing we know: we shall be like Him when He shall appear. Amen! Praise the Lord! We are hoping one day if only we are true and faithful, maybe we shall reach that Home. Pray for me in Jesus's Name.

2. I am glad I can stand here tonight and testify to the blood of Jesus. I am glad for this privilege again to stand. My life is to glorify God. I am thanking God for His wonderful salvation. But for His salvation, brethren, tonight I could not be standing.

He came down and rescued my soul when I was sinking deep in sin. Praise God! He came and delivered me! Praise His Name! Glory be to God! Glory to God! Praise His Name! Glory to God! Praise His Name!

I was at work, and I was reading my Bible there, and I was reading St. Matthew 26. And this verse came to me. It said: 'those that are ready when the bridegroom came and those that are ready shall see God.' These words just rested in my heart, and Jesus come and tell me where they was, and I search my heart and ask God to show me, that when He comes I shall be ready. Praise Him! Praise the Lord! [At this point the testimony is quite drowned by the responses from the congregation.] Pray for me, because my intention is to go along with Jesus.

3. Tonight I can say I am thinking of that glad morning when Christ shall split the blue sky. In His glory we shall see Him coming with all the millions alive. If we are not ready, brethren, we shall not see Him. You know, brethren, we shall see Him but we shall not render Him. You know, brethren, while I was sitting here these words came over to me. 'O what a day! O what a grand and glorious day! O what a happy day! When I shall be with my Lord in Glory to stay.'

There will be no sorrow there. Sin can never enter that place. O praise His Name! You know, brethren, I am thanking God, for sin can't enter there.

So, brethren, the Lord is calling us to be dead unto sin and alive unto righteousness. But, brethren, we are living in these last days when it seems Christians dead too, not realise God is near. Everybody is thinking to do this and to do that. These days when I look at some of the Christians, especially young Christians, I am not speaking young in salvation, just young in age, they are just going as if Jesus has not done nothing for them. Some of them, all they has got is the pleasures of the world taken up in their life, and when you are trying to do your best, they say you are a bit too righteous. Brethren I don't care what they want to say about me, because I got a road before me and it is a narrow road.

I know that on that day I shall be judged. And you know our names shall be called out of the Book of Life, and if our name is not written in that Book of Life and we know that we have not got a lot more time too. So, brethren, pray to the Lord and Christ and get down deeper and deeper in Him until we are wholly lost in Him, until we can't see no more self. Because ourself is a monster. You do everything wicked, but when Jesus is reigning within your life our body is under subjection. So, brethren let us roll the old chariot along and never look behind. And if the Devil in the way we shall roll it over him. And if we see a sinner in the way we shall stop and take them in. Let us be courage and press on, knowing when we shall see Jesus, when He shall split the blue sky, and in His glory we shall Him coming.

Pray for me, brethren, a true soldier. I put my trust in Jesus's name.

APPENDIX VI

TALKING WITH TONGUES

Example 1

'Ɛi ma ma 'majuju 'Ɛi mala ma 'majuju
'Ɛi mama 'matʃə 'maladju 'mamaju
Ɛi mama 'matʃə ju 'mamalu
jujujuju 'mʌməjujuju—Amen Lord.

Example 2

Here each phrase is prefixed by 'He shall be my ——'. This is unusual.

He shall be my amə'jukə
He shall be my 'atandəboinɛ
He shall be my ad'ala 'ʃiləmə 'pandə 'bakə ʃai ba'hikasai
He shall be my 'adai
He shall be my a 'hekobai
He shall be my 'blandə'hopɛn'daləbai
He shall be my da'hokɛn 'saləbai
He shall be my da'Sarəbai
He shall be my da'hokɛntalə 'hokɛntai
He shall be my 'dahokal
He shall be my 'hokɛnsalə 'lipos 'salam
He shall be my 'umbabadalə 'ʃilama

Example 3

'batʃə Kɛn'duri 'hiləmə ma'batʃedu
Amen Jesus! Amen! Amen! Amen Amen! Amen!
'hutʃiləmə ma ma ma'mu 'utʃ
'hiləmə ma ma ma ma ma ma utʃ 'hilə 'hilə
Hallelujah!

APPENDIX VII

PRAYER

1. (At the end of a service.)

ETERNAL Father, we thank Thee for the meeting spent together, we thank You Lord that Your Holy Presence is here with us. We thank Thee for everything that was done this evening. Direct Thy children as we go. Teach us now to pray, help us to come down and humble ourselves before Thee, Lord. Lord make me a soul-winner for Thee. Make me a channel of blessing for Thee, Lord. Crucify myself to the cross with Yourself, O God!

2. (At the beginning of a service.)

Precious God and O Heavenly Father, we thank You tonight dear Jesus that we can gather again one more time in Thy Precious Name. O Lord, we pray Thee O Heavenly Father that You will open the windows of Heaven and that You will pour out Your Spirit, O God. O Lord we beg You this evening that You will take this meeting entirely into Thy hand. And, O God, we ask Thee tonight that even though tongues are so feeble, Heavenly Father, that everything that might be said and done tonight might be to the honour and praise of Thy glory.

Heavenly Father, tonight we pray Thee, O God, that we are here tonight, dear Father, not only to run the congregation. O God, each one tonight might present Thee a soul before Thee, and, O God, You will hide us underneath Thy everlasting wings. Heavenly Father, we ask Thee tonight that You wilt bless every heart, tune every heart by Your Holy Spirit, O God.

And O Lord, tonight when we leave from this place, Heavenly Father, that we will say it was good for us to be here. Heavenly Father we ask Thee. Those because of duty, because of sickness, because of something, dear Father, that they cannot be with us tonight. We ask Thee, O God, that You will give them comfort and let them feel at this moment that somebody, somewhere, is praying for them.

O God, we pray You tonight, You remember the lonely heart. Lord, You will cheer them up. O Lord, You remember this city of London, for Your dear Son name Jesus. Amen.

3. Precious and Eternal Father, bless this evening, O God. Lord Jesus, on Your name we call, thanking Thee Lord for present mercies, Lord, for past mercies. And we thank Thee for the future. Jesus! Jesus! O God, as

I come unto Thee this evening, bless the one that cried unto Thee. Thou art the Lord.

I come unto Thee this evening to keep a deliverance meeting. Lord, I know we are few in number, yet Lord, we know that You have a blessing to give us. As we come to Thee this evening, Lord help us not to be discouraged. Help us to realise, Lord, O God, that in all things we are deep in darkness. Lord Jesus we pray this evening that You will visit this church that is present before Thee.

O Lord Jesus, I pray this evening, O Jesus, that you will make us what You will have us to be. God, cover us with Thy grace this evening. [At this point the prayer was drowned by other voices.]

APPENDIX VIII

PREACHING

Example 1

WITH a clear conscience and we are praying tonight that God as I said oftentimes we are in need of a Holy Ghost revival. I really would not like Bishop ———— to come here and find the church as it is tonight. Individually we say: 'Well, we are making the grade, we are pressing on with the Lord, if the desire of our hearts be true,' but if we are to be honest to our true self, in sight of God, put ourself in the balance, we are found wanting. This is not the time for us to think: 'Well, I am alright in God.' If I was alright in God the revival would break already, and let everyone of us look at it that way. At times it is not my stubborn will or your stubborn will, there is something else, but God wants us to get down, He wants to send multitudes away. The multitudes sometimes keeps us from seeing Jesus, so many multitude, so many different things to do, the multitude in one's life.

You remember those people that wanted to see Jesus, and when they came they said: 'Sirs, we would see Jesus,' and because tonight we mean to see Jesus, to see Jesus, not only to see Him but I want Him to reign again. I ask tonight that he give me a clean heart, a right spirit and, more than all, to revive His work in me. You know what; when I sometimes, there are times I feel I am really going out and other times when I feel I am not really satisfied with this I am. Tonight I am not satisfied with this way I am. I want to be deeper in the Lord, because there are deeper depths and higher heights to go in Christ. As Paul said when he was speaking, I don't remember whether it was the Galatians or Ephesians, he said there are many fillings and we are to seek to be filled each day of our life. The deeper we go in Christ is the deeper the filling becomes in us and the more God can control us and fill us and there we see ourselves daily in God's mirror. You know, you have a glass and you put the glass before your eyes as Paul said. When we are looking through this glass now we see if we are not able to see without it. We see, we go to the mirror and see ourself through the mirror and if our faces are not clean or because they've too much powder, or, if there is something we see what it is. In God's mirror we see what our lives are like, and we must be honest to ourselves, see our weaknesses and ask God to help us to be willing to forsake them.

I feel I want to feel the fire burning. You know some nights when I kneel to pray and when I talk to God and when I tell him myself I feel I

am nothing in His sight. I think Paul said to St. Peter once: 'Mind you!
when you think you are something you are nothing,' and when you fee,
that you are something and you are just nothing in His sight, and Peter
said these words that: 'The best we do is lighter than vanity,' and what is
vanity? it is nothing!

. . . Sometime half-past twelve I gone to bed, sometime half-past one,
but there I get up and talk to the Lord, because when He appear to me the
other morning He said: 'Tell the people I am coming again.' And brethren,
whether we believe it or not the Second Coming of Christ is very near, and
He is coming for a prepared people, a people without spot and wrinkle.
And He said He is going to wash us whiter than snow. You know those
words make a deep impression on my heart. Do you know when snow is
falling in its pure form, without any dust getting into it, you know how
pure and clean it is. It is a blessing in our souls.

O now we see that cleansing stream. You know that stream of blood
that come from His side. We plunge and it cleanseth us. It cleanseth us
from sin. Three days now I notice the Devil has set at my hour of prayer.
At five to twelve each day I go down in prayer until ten past, and I go back
to my desk and as I am writing I am praying to God. Brother and sister
(it makes no difference) we are going to be His waiting brides.

Example 2

Blessed be the reading of His holy Word. Amen. Praise God. Well, you
see, dear ones, this chapter has got so much in it . . . praise and deliverance
message. As we look here at Jesus passed through the cornfield on the
sabbath He could see that the scribes and the Pharisees were watching
Him, but when He met this man with the withered hand He healed him.
The word of God says in the tenth verse that his hand was healed.

And today there are so many suffering without realising that Jesus is the
cure. But you know the Christians are falling so much from their Saviour,
what could you expect from the world? I met a brother somewhere this
evening and I said to him: 'Brother, what has happened to you, I didn't
see you come.'

He said he was in the hospital, he had an illness in his head and he was
taken away over the other side of London. And I said to him, I said:
'Brother, we are having a deliverance meeting, come up for prayer,' and
he said he would come.

You know we should look into the Christian world today. Christians
need deliverance just as much as the world. I met another real worker for
God during the week and when I went to see him, he said to me: 'Why
have you come?' I said: 'I was led to come.' I never saw that brother for
more than a year but I was led to come. He said: 'I have been praying to
God here for weeks now, to see a proper preacher, because when I see in
what is taking place; the churches are going wrong.'

When we look around and see Christians doing various things, how can the world be delivered when we want deliverance? In three to four months there are about four Pentecostal churches in . . . that have gone flat, flat, flat, flat! smashed to pieces all because of men that have tried to have their own way for years and years. And they have been warned and the time come when they just couldn't go farther. And I remember one of the very ministers, I warned him some times ago. I said: 'Brother, if you don't keep God's will you are not going to go too far.'

They rejected me, they despised me, they did this and they did that and I live to see that their work have come to nought. I can't rejoice over it. We see that the world must be delivered, but the church must be delivered first. Amen. And I am taking God at His word. I believe every promise that He has made. I still believe that God is going to give us a revival, but He want us to have some experiences first. [At this point I have omitted a long exposition of the story of the Tower of Babel.]

God is going to confound the Christians so much today that when they finally are confounded and split up and split up, then they are going to ask God what is the matter. Then He can reveal Himself and say: 'You have not been walking according to the Scripture.' Praise God! and He has started it. God is confounding the people now. They must be confused. Amen!

Imagine! one sister had a nice church, a real woman of God, and just because she flourished with money she dashed to Jamaica, she dashed to America, and she come back home with a bishop. He don't believe in no baptism whatsoever. He's a coloured man. From America. He don't believe in no baptism, no water baptism now. He says it is not necessary in this age. What you want is a baptism of the Holy Ghost and fire. They are starting their convention tomorrow. And that erroneous thing the man has come back with, it smashed the church to pieces. If they won't believe the truth God is going to send them a strong delusion. [At this point the preacher's voice was drowned by expressions of assent from the congregation.]

Do let us keep holding the fort, because God is on the job. Imagine a man that has been in the Pentecostal faith for years come to the point now that water baptism is not necessary, only the baptism of the Holy Ghost and fire.

And this is how he interpret it. He said that John said that he was baptising with water, but the one that was coming after was greater, and He would baptise with the Holy Ghost and fire. So he is neither concerned about baptism in the titles, or baptism in the name. He don't want nothing at all. He don't want the Lord's Supper. All those things he has cut out and yet the name of the movement is the Gospel of Light and Truth Church of God.

APPENDIX IX

CHORUSES

THESE examples are favourites. The only collection I know of, cyclostyled sheets in use in a Jesus Name sect, contains a hundred and thirty, but many of these are seldom heard. The one verse is repeated over and over again.

Hallelujah, Hallelujah, Hallelujah, by and by,
    Hallelujah, Hallelujah, we will meet Him in the sky,
Hallelujah, Hallelujah, there the loved ones never die,
    Hallelujah, glory Hallelujah, blessed Hallelujah, by and by.

I shall not, I shall not be moved,
    I shall not, I shall not be moved,
Like a tree that's planted by the waters,
    I shall not be moved.

He lifted me, He lifted me,
    Jesus came along and He lifted me,
From my load of sin I now am free,
    Hallelujah, Jesus lifted me.

My Bible and I, my Bible and I,
    What a wonderful treasure,
God's gift without measure,
    We will travel together,
My Bible and I.

Yes! He is mine, yes! He is mine,
    Joy in my soul, peace in my mind,
Yes! He is mine, yes! He is mine,
    Jesus alone is mine.

Isaiah prophesied, Isaiah prophesied,
    Behold! the virgin shall bear a child,
His name shall be called the Mighty God,
    The Everlasting Father and the Prince of Peace.

SELECT BIBLIOGRAPHY

THE literature of religious movements is immense and a great deal of it is relevant to the consideration of West Indian sects in England. Similar phenomena occur, or have occurred in nearly every part of the world under what are, very broadly, similar circumstances. Race and intergroup relations also has a vast and growing body of literature. For these reasons I have listed only those works from which I have drawn information directly, those which I am conscious have influenced my analysis and some which contain specialist bibliographies of the fields with which they deal.

F. R. Augier and S. C. Gordon, *Sources of West Indian History*, London, Longmans, Green & Co., 1962.

F. R. Augier, S. C. Gordon, D. G. Hall and M. Reckord, *The Making of the West Indies*, London, Longmans, 1960.

S. Barton Babbage, *Hau-Hauism: An Episode in the Maori Wars*, Wellington, A. H. and A. W. Reed, 1937.

Michael Banton, *White and Coloured*, London, Jonathan Cape, 1959.

Michael Banton, *The Coloured Quarter*, London, Jonathan Cape, 1955.

Roger Bastide, *Les Religions africaines au Brésil*, Paris, Presses Universitaires de France, 1960.

Fredrik Barth, *Political Leadership Among the Swat Pathans*, L.S.E. Monographs on Social Anthropology, No. 19, London, Athlone Press, 1959.

E. D. Beynon, 'The Voodoo Cult Among Negro Migrants in Detroit', *American Journal of Sociology*, July 1937–May 1938.

Clinton V. Black, *A History of Jamaica*, London and Glasgow, Collins, 1958.

Judith Blake, *Family Structure in Jamaica: the Social Context of Reproduction*, New York, The Free Press of Glencoe, 1961.

K. O. L. Burridge, *Mambu—a Melanesian Millennium*, London, Methuen, 1960.

M. J. C. Calley, 'Bandjalang Social Organisation', Unpublished Ph.D. Thesis, University of Sydney.

Gertrude Carmichael, *The History of the West Indian Islands of Trinidad and Tobago*, London, Alvin Redman, 1961.

Church of God Preacher, a publication (intermittent) of the Church of God of Prophecy, Bedford, June 1961.

Edith Clarke, *My Mother who Fathered Me*, London, George Allen and Unwin, 1957.

Norman Cohn, *The Pursuit of the Millennium*, London, Mercury Books (Heinemann), 1962.

Sydney Collins, *Coloured Minorities in Britain*, London, Lutterworth, 1957.

Charles W. Conn, *Like a Mighty Army Moves the Church of God*, Cleveland, Church of God Publishing House, 1955.

Philip D. Curtin, *The Two Jamaicas*, Cambridge, Mass., Harvard University Press, 1955.

R. B. Davison, *West Indian Migrants—Social and Economic Facts of Migration from the West Indies*, London, Oxford University Press for the Institute of Race Relations, 1962.

R. B. Davison, *Commonwealth Immigrants*, London, Oxford University Press for the Institute of Race relations, 1964 (a useful survey, published after the present work was written).

Emile Durkheim, *The Elementary Forms of the Religious Life*, trans. J. W. Swain, New York, Collier Books, 1961.

David Edwards, *Report on an Economic Study of Small Farming in Jamaica*, Institute of Social and Economic Research, University College of the West Indies, Glasgow, The University Press, 1961.

E. Franklin Frazier, *The Negro Church in America*, Liverpool, Liverpool University Press, 1964 (this came to hand too late to influence what I have written—an excellent study).

R. Firth (Ed.), *Man and Culture—an Evaluation of the Work of Bronislaw Malinowski*, London, Routledge and Kegan Paul, 1957.

Donald Gee, *The Pentecostal Movement*, London, Elim Publishing Company, 2nd ed., 1949.

Ruth Glass, *Newcomers, the West Indians in London*, Centre for Urban Studies, London, George Allen and Unwin, 1960.

Max Gluckman, *The Judicial Process among the Barotse of Northern Rhodesia*, Manchester, Manchester University Press for the Rhodes-Livingstone Institute, 1955.

Max Gluckman, *Custom and Conflict in Africa*, Oxford, Basil Blackwell, 1959.

Daniel Guérin, *The West Indies and Their Future* (trans. A. Wainhouse), London, Dennis Dobson, 1961.

Clifford S. Hill, *Black and White in Harmony*, London, Hodder and Stoughton, 1958.

Clifford S. Hill, *West Indian Migrants and the London Churches*, London, Oxford University Press for the Institute of Race Relations, 1963.

F. M. Henriques, *Family and Colour in Jamaica*, London, Eyre and Spottiswoode, 1953.

Frances S. Herskovitz and J. Melville, *Trinidad Village*, New York, A. A. Knopf, 1947.

Anthony Jackson, *The Irish in Britain*, London, Routledge and Kegan Paul, 1963.

H. James and Cora Tenen, *The Teacher was Black*, London, Heinemann, 1953.

Chandra Jayawardena, *Conflict and Solidarity in a Guianese Plantation*, L.S.E. Monographs on Social Anthropology, No. 25, London, Athlone Press, 1963.

Bishop Johnson, *Who is it that Defies and Challenges the Whole Religious World on these Subjects?* Philadelphia, 1958, no publisher.

C. E. Lincoln, *The Black Muslims in America*, Boston, Beacon Press, 1961.

K. L. Little, *Negroes in Britain*, London, Routledge and Kegan Paul, 1955.

Raymond Mack and Richard Snyder, *The Analysis of Social Conflict: Conflict Resolution*, Vol. I, June 1957, pp. 212–47.

Mona Macmillan, *The Land of Look Behind*, London, Faber and Faber, 1957.

Douglas Manley, 'The Formal Associations of a Negro Community in Britain', *Social and Economic Studies*, Vol. 4, 1955, pp. 231–44.

P. Mason (ed.), *Man, Race and Darwin*, London, Oxford University Press for the Institute of Race Relations, 1960.

N. Verrle McCullough, *The Negro in English Literature*, Ilfracombe (Devon), A. H. Stockwell, 1962.

J. G. Moore, 'The Religion of Jamaican Negroes', unpublished Ph.D. thesis, North-western University, *circa* 1954.

Eyo B. N'dem, 'The Statue of Coloured People in Britain', *Phylon*, Vol. XVIII, 1957, pp. 82–7.

Eyo B. N'dem, *Negro Immigrants in Manchester*, unpublished M.A. Thesis, University of Manchester.

Katrin Norris, *Jamaica: the Search for an Identity*, London, Oxford University Press for the Institute of Race Relations, 1962.

Lord Olivier, *The Myth of Governor Eyre*, Hogarth Press, London, 1933.

Lord Olivier, *Jamaica, the Blessed Island*, Faber and Faber, London, 1936.

Sheila Patterson, *Dark Strangers*, London, Tavistock Publications, 1963.

Janet Reid, 'Negro Workers in Manchester', *Sociological Review*, Vol. 4, 1956, pp. 199–211.

A. H. Richmond, *Colour Prejudice in Britain*, London, Routledge and Kegan Paul, 1954.

James H. Robb, *Working-Class Anti-Semite*, London, Tavistock Publications, 1954.

Elliott M. Rudwick, *W. E. B. Du Bois: A Study in Minority Group Leadership*, Philadelphia, University of Pennsylvania Press, 1960.

C. Senior and D. Manley, *A Report on Jamaican Migration to Great Britain*, Kingston, Government Publications, 1955.

Muzafer Sherif (ed.), *Intergroup Relations and Leadership*, New York, John Wiley and Sons for the University of Oklahoma Institute of Intergroup Relations, 1962.

George Eaton Simpson, 'Jamaican Revivalist Cults', *Social and Economic Studies*, Vol. V, No. 4, University College of the West Indies, 1956.

M. G. Smith, R. Augier and R. Nettleford, *The Ras Tafari Movement*, Institute of Social and Economic Research, University College of the West Indies, 1960.

M. G. Smith, *Kinship and Community in Cariacou*, New Haven and London, Yale University Press, 1962.

Raymond T. Smith, *The Negro Family in British Guiana*, London, Routledge and Kegan Paul, 1956.

Bengt Sundkler, *Bantu Prophets in South Africa* (2nd ed.), London, Oxford University Press for the International African Institute, 1961.

J. Wickenden, *Colour in Britain*, London, Oxford University Press for the Institute of Race Relations, 1958.

Eric Williams, *History of the Peoples of Trinidad and Tobago*, Port of Spain, P.N.M., 1962.

Robin M. Williams, Jr., 'Religion, Value Orientations and Intergroup Conflict', *The Journal of Social Issues*, Vol. XII, No. 3, 1955.

Francesca Wilson, *They Came as Strangers*, London, Hamish Hamilton, 1959.

Bryan R. Wilson, *Sects and Society*, London, Heinemann, 1961.

Donald Wood (ed.), *Coloured Immigrants in Britain*, London, Oxford University Press for the Institute of Race Relations, 1960.

Peter Worsley, *The Trumpet Shall Sound*, London, MacGibbon and Kee, 1957.

J. M. Yinger (ed.), *Religion, Society and the Individual*, New York, Macmillan Company, 1957. See especially contributions by Max Weber, J. B. Bolt, R. R. Dynes, W. Mueldor, L. Pope, A. H. Fauset, G. E. Simpson, W. D. Wallis, W. E. Garrison, R. M. Williams, E. T. Cark and E. Trooltsch.

INDEX